Imprisoned In A Body With A Life Sentence

Deborah Duffield

Order this book online at www.trafford.com/07-0038
or email orders@trafford.com

Most Trafford titles are also available at major online book retailers.

Note for Librarians: A cataloguing record for this book is available from Library and Archives Canada at www.collectionscanada.ca/amicus/index-e.html

ISBN: 978-1-4251-1629-3

We at Trafford believe that it is the responsibility of us all, as both individuals and corporations, to make choices that are environmentally and socially sound. You, in turn, are supporting this responsible conduct each time you purchase a Trafford book, or make use of our publishing services. To find out how you are helping, please visit www.trafford.com/responsiblepublishing.html

Our mission is to efficiently provide the world's finest, most comprehensive book publishing service, enabling every author to experience success. To find out how to publish your book, your way, and have it available worldwide, visit us online at www.trafford.com/10510

www.trafford.com

North America & international
toll-free: 1 888 232 4444 (USA & Canada)
phone: 250 383 6864 • fax: 250 383 6804 • email: info@trafford.com

The United Kingdom & Europe
phone: +44 (0)1865 487 395 • local rate: 0845 230 9601
facsimile: +44 (0)1865 481 507 • email: info.uk@trafford.com

10 9 8 7 6 5 4 3

Contents

Introduction

I am writing this book so that other people can understand what I went through, and for my own healing. Everything that happened to me is real and true, and I did not butter it up. This is heart wrenching for some people to read, but it is accurate and not fiction. I would like also to applaud all the survivors for their strength and willingness to change their lives for the better and not allow what happened to them in the past be in their future like I did. 45 years it has taken me to live, not just survive, I call that a great accomplishment and I am proud of myself. I am proud of all the other survivors that have been able to do the same, pulling themselves out of that vicious circle. I am also proud of the survivors that are trying, it is not easy, and it takes time, just have some hope, and it will come.

Sexual abuse has happened to many people, boys, and girls, age does not matter, and there is no prejudice to perpetrators. Perpetrator's can be preachers, doctors, lawyers, nurses, mothers, fathers, brothers, sisters, or a complete stranger or anyone else for that matter, even different nationalities. That is the worst of this crime. It can happen in an old deserted house, outside, in a restaurant washroom, in a barn, anywhere. It can even happen in your own home.

Little children cannot do anything to protect themselves when they are small, but the words they say when they are older, "I should have done something", but that is not the reality. They could not do any thing about it. What I would like to do is try to stop it. Teach the children it is not right and against the law for anyone to touch any part of them, that is your private parts. Ask our preachers to have a sermon on this subject. Not once did I hear about this at church, and I went a lot.

We have the right to have respect, be loved and cared for as a child, to me there is no compromise, and children cannot defend themselves. Myself as an adult, I will defend a child to the end. I lost a lot of my life do to FEAR. I do not want to see anyone else lose his or hers. Every time I hear something on the TV and Internet, in the news about children being mistreated or demoralized, it just makes me sick and angry to hear of all the pain and suffering that the children have to go through before they can be heard. What are people thinking? This question, I cannot answer.

I am hoping my story will give hope to others and let them know there is a way to heal. It is hard, and you have to want to change. Not just say it, but also participate in your change. No one can do it but you. You do have it in you; you just have to work at it.

When Innocence Should Have Been Treasured

My life began at age 3 1/2. Before this time, I did not know who I was or where I came from, but I was placed in a family that was supposed to love me. This lady from the children's services brought me in and said;" this is your new mommy and daddy". I looked at them and started to cry. Where did my mommy and daddy go? She immediately said, this will be your new home they are nice people you will like them. That did not help me much. They changed my name so that was confusing. Half the time I did not know they where talking to me. I cried for almost 2 weeks, my mother told me. My new mother did not know what to do with me, so she told my father to deal with me. He came in and lay down on the bed, and held on to me until I fell asleep. After I had stopped crying and got to know them, I did not think they were too bad. They let me play run around the house and introduced me to my new brother. He was bigger than I was. I do not think he liked me much.

I met my new grandfather and he was wonderful. I just loved him. I sat on his knee, and he always gave me candy, tickled me, and made me feel happy. Not long after he passed away from tuberculosis. He was special to me. Now another one in my life was gone. He made me happy. Later on, we went to his grave. I looked up, and who did I see, my grandpa. I turned white as a ghost and passed out. When I came to, my mother and aunt were there by my side, and they were laughing, they said; do not be scared that's grandpa's brother our uncle. Boy did he ever look like grandpa. That was a relief to me because; I could not understand how he got from under the ground to on top.

One Day my father and mother had decided to go for a ride out into the country. We stopped at this great big farmhouse with a barn across the road. I am all excited. I have room to run and play. I looked around, and the neighbours were so far away. It is not like being in the city, where the neighbours are right next door to you. There is a big field in between the neighbours, and us. I did not know if there were kids next door, so I didn't know who I would be able to play with.

Moving day came. I was excited, as children should be. We got to the new house. I ran up one set of stairs and down the other, sat on the stairs, and bumping all way down laughing. This was so much fun I thought this was great until Mom and Dad told me to get outside, because I was in the way. So where did I go, the woodshed, climbing over wood then to the barn checking everything out and having a wonderful time.

I finally have freedom from the city with all the noise of the cars and close neighbours. There is so much out in the country to be able to do when you're a child, running yelling, laughing, watching the birds, climbing the trees as far as I can. The world was in my hands, and I could do anything, so I thought. Not knowing what was ahead. We eventually found out that there were twin girls down the road from us.

My father came in the house one day and said" mother, we need a wood stove in the kitchen to cook on" she said that would be nice, so they went out and bought a wood cook stove for in the kitchen. I remember mother being very happy when she could bake in it. In addition, it was so nice to be able to stand over by it and get warm and cozy, we already had a wood furnace that kept the house warm on the main floor, and there was no heat up stairs. It was a two-floor farmhouse with a basement with a dirt floor, five rooms upstairs, and four rooms on the main floor. This is the layout; Kitchen, living room, pantry, dinning room, and a bedroom/study with an attached summer kitchen at the back of the house, and the dreaded woodshed. When you went upstairs and turned to your right, there was one little room on your left. For a while, I was in that little room but that was not long for me and then you go down the hall and a bigger room, which was my Mom and Dads bedroom. Now, if you turn to your left at the stairs instead of going right, you would go through a big room that was my brother's, and then through a smaller room and then the smallest room in the house. That room was mine for the rest of the time I lived there.

A little while went by; dad had to buy a tractor in order to bring the wood from the forest up to the house. This is when things started to happen.

My Life Was Changing

Dad said "Dub" that is what he called me, how would you like to go for a ride on the tractor with me? Yes! Jumping up and down yes, I was excited. This would be my first tractor ride. Mom said she is a little small to ride on it. Dad said no! I will watch her, so off we went down the very long laneway to the woods. It was a bumpy ride but a lot of fun. I didn't even fall off the tractor

When we got there, Dad was cutting down trees and I of course was playing with bugs and frogs, the good stuff, you know. I ran to my dad, I have to go number one this is what they told us we had to say and number 2 for the other. His response was, go in the bush behind a tree. I can't, I will get in trouble. He assured me, that I would not get in trouble. Just go behind the tree and go, so I did. When I came back out my T-shirt and shirt was out, well that is not good; he said we have to tuck that in. We cannot have you running around with your shirt out, come here, and let Daddy tuck it in properly for you. He lifted me up on the trailer and pulled my pants down and his fingers went inside. I didn't know what he was doing. I gasped. Do not be scared he would say. I am tickling your tummy you're going to like it. Did you not know you had a hole there? That is where all daddies get to tickle their little girls. Does every one have it? I ask. Yes, even mommy has one and daddy tickles mommy there too. He did this to me, for years not knowing it was wrong. Then he tucks my shirt in, this is how you put your shirt inside your pants. I didn't know what to say it did not make me laugh, but when we got back to the house, I ran inside, Mom, mom, Daddy tickled me inside. She said, what do you mean? Daddy put His finger inside! He put it in my PP and tickled my tummy. She looked up and said to my father. What did you do? He said. My finger slipped when I was tucking in her shirt. That is all.

I guess she believed him, because it never came up again. This happened on a daily basis. He would come into my room at night when he was not at work to check on me. He told mom that he heard me up, and he would put his fingers in there again.

I would stay awake as long as I could so I could hear him coming and I would pretend that I was sleeping, but I think he knew I wasn't. When I went to school, I fell asleep during class, many times. Believe me; the teacher didn't like it either.

He would take me to the barn and rub his penis up against me and white stuff would come out. What is that? Oh, do not worry about that, you will know soon enough! All Daddies have to do this to teach their kids things that they have to know. I will be showing you many things, so you will know them when you are old enough, like what you are supposed to do with your husband when you get married. However, that will be a long way off.

He said; "I should have started teaching you a long time ago but you had to come in to our home first".

My father would fondle me and play his little games. I found out later in life, they call it oral sex; he performed on me, not me on him. I just thought it was normal for him to do these things to me, because I had no one else to tell me any different.

It was time to start a new school. It was a one-room schoolhouse. The teacher was mean; she hit my hands with a ruler. Threw books at us, punched, kicked, and made us stand in a corner with a dunce hat on. Some students mostly the bad apples did not get a chance to go to the bathroom during school hours only at lunch or recess. I would end up going number 1 in my pants and get the strap for that. She would have the whole class laughing at whoever it was, as she pointed us out; I didn't think it was very funny.

My father came to the school, and told the teacher that if she gave me the strap, to call and he would give me the strap at home as well. It did not take long for me to learn what was going to happen. The first day I got the strap at school for asking for an eraser from the kid next to me. Then she called home and told my father or mother. When I got home, I got the strap and sent to bed without getting dinner. Mom brought me up some food when Dad was not around. I ended up going to bed without supper many a night and dad would not allow mom to bring me any food, if she was there.

When I would get the strap at home, it was not the same as at school. At school, the strap went halfway up my arm, and I had a big red welt from it. At home, he would pull down my pants, put me over his knee, put my legs between his legs, and start beating on me until I cried. That would go on until I was crying hysterically and could not breathe. Then he would stop and if I cried, more than five minutes after he stopped beating me he would say, stop the crying, or I will give you more to cry about, and if I didn't stop crying he would start all over again and saying, you know, this is hurting me more than it is you. I didn't understand how it could be hurting him more than it did me. He would say this after every beating.

This went on every day in my life sometimes twice in one day. Some days, I didn't know why I was getting the strap but I did. I used to be upset in the mornings and say to my mother that I don't want to go to school. She beats us all up, and then when I come home, I would get beat up again by Dad. My mother knew this was happening, but could never do anything about it because, my father had put fear into my mother, and she was a victim too.

One time the teacher went to a student's home. She went in to their house, pulled him out of bed. The mother running and screaming behind her saying, the boy's father just died, leave him alone he is sick. The teacher never listened and threw him in the back of her car, he is in pyjamas, drove to the school and pulled him out of the back seat and threw him on the ground. Then she began kicking him, screaming at him. Get up, quit your faking, your mother may believe you, but I don't, you're just a little loser. In my mind, I was thinking the teacher is just like my father.

The teacher would keep me after school, because I was either bad or I didn't have my homework from the night before done right so, I would get a beating at home for being late and grounded, and the strap at school for not having my homework done right. I could not win no matter what I did. This is when I started thinking this is not how I like to feel. I felt sad all the time, I wasn't happy any more and seeing people was not fun.

It was my father's fault, my homework was not done right, my father would say he would help me but he never helped me, he did the homework himself. He did it for me, because he said I was too stupid to do it. I didn't have the brains or gumption to do anything right, and he was not going to look bad just because I was stupid. I would take my homework to school, it was all wrong, and I would get the strap at school for having it wrong. I tried to tell the teacher that my dad did my homework, but she started yelling at me saying," Do you think that I am that stupid to think your father did this work, and it's wrong? I do not think so." So, out came the strap, one for lying, and one for not doing my homework right. What it boils down to is I would get the strap, no matter what happened at home or school. It didn't matter. A person can only handle so much of this, day after day. When I went home my hands would be sore from getting the strap at school and when I went to school, my butt would be sore from the beatings at home. He made sure that I did not have any bruises, so no one would know what was going on. I started going #1 in my pants, having nightmares, staying awake at night, and being afraid of people.

Now, he is stepping it up a little more. He had me go to the barn, where he showed me how he would kill a kitten. He turns to me, as he is wringing the little kitten's head off. I will do this to you if you continue telling people that I do things to you, because I will deny it and they will think that you are lying.

What I did was tell a friend at school, what my father was doing, her reply to me was, it was happening to her too from her stepfather. She told me she would help by hiding in the bushes taking a picture and that way I could take it to the police and have him charged. This is when I knew it was against the law what he was doing, when she said, the Police could get involved; When I came to her later on, that week she told me she could not do it. She only said it to make me feel better, that it never really happened to her. I never talked to her again. I thought she had lied to me or told my father what I had said.

Now I am terrified, because he is bigger than I am. In addition, I could be killed, he has told me so, and I believe him. I have also seen him go after my brother with an axe handle beating him. I ran over and screamed at him leave my brother alone, he responded, you get out of here or you will get the same, I took off running.

I am feeling everything is hopeless. My stomach was churning. I started getting headaches; I could not let my parents know that I was feeling sick; they would not have believed me, anyway. I didn't know what to do about what was happening. I had nowhere to turn, and nowhere to go, no one to help me; I believed no one really cared anyway. I could not understand; why anyone wanted to live like this, and have to go through this, it was not worth it. He had all sorts of guns and knives, they were locked in the gun holder except for his knives, but he could still get them out and use them, my biggest fear.

I was laying on the floor petting our cat when he came in with a 22 hand gun it went off just missing me and going into the cat, and then into the floor. I jumped up screaming, there was blood everywhere. He shot through his hand. I did not know it had passed the bridge of my nose until mom came out of the bathroom, she came running out, what happened. Dad said, the gun accidentally went off and through my hand. She said, Deb you have blood on your nose and Dad responded by saying, It's the blood from my hand, we have to go to the hospital, he said, Dub, you have to change gears, and I will drive. My mother never had a driver's license and didn't know how to drive; I knew how to change gears. When we got to the hospital, we went in, they asked, did the bullet hit you, because you have blood on your face. He spoke up no, she fell and hit her nose on the table. He covered his tracks. I didn't dare tell them that I was lying on the floor beside the cat; the bullet went through the cat and in to the floor. I feel he was trying to kill me, and tried to make it look like an accident. They cleaned up the wound on my nose and said that it really doesn't look like a scrape caused from a fall, but Dad insisted that's what happened. They fixed his hand, and off we went back home, but we never made it all the way home; he had to stop and do his little fatherly duties.

I started in my next year of school, hoping things would be better, but it continued. A cousin came over and asked my dad if I could have this little puppy, it was a beagle. It was so cute I loved it. My father replied. Yes, she can have the puppy. I was so happy I play with the puppy. I got up for school on Monday morning, and my father informed me to get someone to take puppy, I could not keep it. I knew I had to get someone that would love the puppy, so when I went to school, I asked all the kids, and one said she could have the puppy. She was a nice girl, so I knew the puppy was going to a good home. I could hardly wait until lunchtime, I ran home for lunch as fast as I could, to tell my father the puppy had a new home. As I was coming into view of our house, I seen my father put the little puppy down, back up, point the gun, and shoot him before I could reach him. I stopped running; the little puppy lay dead. When I got up to him, Dad said, you were not fast enough and this could be you so just remember this. I didn't dare cry, all he said was, now bury it. As I was burying the little puppy, I was wishing it were my father that I was burying and not the puppy.

A new teacher started that year, which made me very happy. She was nice, friendly, and even talked to me. That was unusual, because no one talked to me, no one liked me, I thought. She approached my parents about getting glasses. She felt that I could not see properly and that was why I did so poorly in school. My father and mother took me to the eye doctor. My father was so upset he said," you only want glasses; because all of us have glasses and you want attention that's all it is".

When the glasses came in, I wore them maybe two days. I didn't like wearing them. He grabbed and smashed them and told mom and the teacher that I broke them, and he was not about to buy another pair. That ended wearing glasses. The teacher caught on to my father very quickly and knew that he had a temper. This teacher was fantastic. I thought maybe that I would get some help. Things are going to change for the better.

This teacher, she sat with me, talked with me, and was showing me how to do some of the lessons we had done that day. I did not do homework anymore, well very seldom. I did it with the teacher. This was great but as time went on things got worse at home. My father would give me heck, thinking I was lying, because I was not bringing my homework home to do. He thought I was just refusing to bring it home, but that was not the case. He told the teacher the same as the previous teacher. If I got the strap at school, phone him. The teacher told him she would not be giving me the strap. In addition, she would not phone when or if she did give me the strap. She was such a cool teacher. I only received the strap once from her. That was because I told her, She was a flea, and I was laughing, it was a dare from the other students saying I was too chicken to tell her that. She did not hit me hard matter of fact, we were both laughing, and then she call me nut. That year was the first time in my life; I passed with B, B+, and an A. It was usually an F or D- that is what my dad said; F for failed and D for dumbest, I never did see a report card before, I was never allowed opening any envelope or I would get the strap. I could never to do anything.

This teacher was so nice that when the Christmas party came up, she went to my father and asked if I could go. He said, no! She is not going to those things. It was against his moral judgment, what ever that meant, and I was too unruly to be out at functions. She waited a while and asked my parents again only in a different way. She asked if she could pick me up and tutor me for the night and they agreed. She had asked me not to tell and I knew how to keep a secret. So I never did tell. I was so excited I was able to go to the Christmas party after all. My father and mother were at a prayer meeting, and on their way home, they decided to stop at the hall, where there were many cars outside. They saw the car she drove and caught me. My father yelled and screamed at the teacher and said he would never trust her again. This was in front of everyone, the kids, and their parents. I knew when I got home; there would be hell to pay. He hit me in the head, kicked me, gave me the belt, sent me to bed, and I was grounded. I could not go anywhere anyway. The next day the teacher came to me and apologized. I told her I knew it was too good to be true at least she tried, and I did have fun, even if it was for a short time. This was the first and only year I ever passed my grade, with B's & A's.

The school down the road from mine was for grades five to eight. My school only went to grade four. An older boy from the school down the road came to me, said your brother wants some help, and asked me to come with him. I went with him, but my brother was nowhere around. I don't think he went to school there, he just lived by it, and did cleaning with his mother. He took me in to the school and said my brother was in the boy's bathroom, I said, I would wait for him out here. He then pulled me in to the bathroom, and pulled out a knife and said pull your pants down. I knew what was happening, so I did. I had my legs tight together. He said "you let me do this, or I will kill your dad" That made me happy, my reply was that's all right go-ahead kill him. He does the same thing you're doing. He said; he would kill my mother and brother. That is when I gave in; I did not want them killed.

He attempted to do this on several occasions. Sometimes he couldn't because there were too many people around, but then there were times, when there was no one around, and I got raped again. He was so bold, he came in the out-house and held me at knifepoint, and my parents saw him coming and came out. They said, come out of there. As we came out, he was holding a knife to my throat and said to my parents, if you say anything to anybody, I will kill her, no matter where she is. My parents said nothing; they didn't even phone the police. When I asked my father, why didn't you do something? His reply, what was I supposed to do; I am not that stupid to get your mother and I killed. You likely invited him here and he was covering for you. I knew immediately that I had no protection from anything. The boy continued to do this until I left home for good.

When I saw him coming, I would run and hide, it was when I didn't see him coming that I was in trouble.

Started In To Puberty A Month Before My Ninth Birthday

My underwear was missing from the laundry. Mom went upstairs to find them, but she couldn't find them, she asked me, Where are your underwear? I said, I don't know, I knew very well where they were. Then my brother got involved, thinking he would get me in trouble, and searched my closet, where he found them. Running down the stairs, he is yelling she went #1 in her pants again and hid them, I found them in her closet under a bunch of toys. I was frightened, and started shaking and thought, here we go again; I knew I was in trouble, but to my surprise mom didn't yell or get mad at me, instead, she told my brother to go watch TV. Then she went in to my grandmas' room. She was in there a while. Then she came out and said I want you to talk to your grandma. I was puzzled; I didn't know why she wasn't mad. Grandma was living with us by this time, my dad's mother. She was my rock. She made me feel like a person and her most famous saying was. "Debbie, you can do anything you want and be any thing you want". She was nothing like her son quite the opposite.

Grandma sat me down and explained to me that I had my women's monthly problem. Not to be afraid, it was natural, but I had to put on this special pad, so it would not go on my panties. That was a relief. I didn't go #1 in my pants, but this was much worse to me. She asked me why I hid them and I told her, I thought I had wet my pants, and she began to laugh. My mother took me to the doctor, because she did not know why I had started so young. The doctor said that I am starting at a very young age and it was unusual to be this young and informed them, my breasts were growing as well. When I went to school, sometimes I would pass out from the pain caused by my period, and teacher would lay me down on the cot. She would never call my parents, because she knew what would happen when I got home.

The following year, we had another new teacher and she was nice, and I never received the strap from her. Unbelievably, I had a crush on her maybe crush is not the right word, but it works for me. I wanted her to be my mother. She was so cool and passionate she never raised her voice, but she got her message across, when things were wrong. She would hug me, even others too.

This is when I started thinking on ways to get back at my father, and maybe break free from the torture. I didn't lie to my father; anything I said was a lie to him, anyway, even if it was the truth. One-time for two years I was to stay home and not go out anywhere, because I was five minutes late coming home from school. I received the strap, sent to bed without supper, and on top of all that my homework taken away so I could not finish it. I started to cry hysterically and said to my mom what is the use I can't do any thing, I don't want to live here, send me back to children services, I don't want to do this anymore, this isn't the way I want to live, and from that day on I never saw a reason to live. I started to steal money from dad and buy things the kids had at school. One of them came to the house and said your daughter bought this pencil case from my daughter for $20. Dad turned around and asked me, and where did you get the money? My reply, out of your wallet, you are lying, I am not missing any money out of my wallet, (I thought maybe they would send me to a detention center, that didn't work), but all I got was the strap sent to bed with no supper, the usual. Then I tried saying, I killed someone, maybe this would work, It didn't they just thought I was looking for attention. I had heard some other kids talking, that so and so had killed someone and they went to a detention center and I thought it would work for me, but it didn't because I really didn't kill anyone. I would get in to fights at school, after school, whenever I could, so they would send me away or give me back to children services but that didn't work either. I had two options left, live with it, or hope that he would kill me quickly and soon or kill myself. I knew the day would come when rage that was inside of me would come out, and I would kill him or he would kill me. It was inevitable.

I was sitting at the kitchen table waiting for supper, and my father came in and we always had prayer before we ate. Then mom had to serve dad first, then my brother, then me and last herself. On this particular evening, we were having liver and onions, my mother, and I did not like this, but my father insisted we have it. My father was eating and liked it very much, and my brother as well, but when I was eating it I started to gag; my father started to yell at me. You stop that right now. I couldn't. It came back up he reach across and smacked me in the face. You are going to eat it, if it's the last thing on earth. Then he grabbed a hold of me and started shoving it back into my mouth, which only caused me to gag even more, and it came back up. I was choking, but that didn't stop him. He kept yelling you are going to eat this. Then my mom stepped in and said, stop this. He did and I had to go to bed with no supper again. Another time, a similar incident happened when I got sick, he made me eat my own puke. My grandma was there at that time, and she stopped him. She told him this was ridiculous, how he was acting, if she doesn't like it she doesn't have to eat it. He went in to a rage on his mother and that made me feel bad because it was over me that he was screaming at her. I was afraid for my grandma, that he might hit her; she was very frail.

Now I Am Imprisoned In This Body And Life

I hated myself, who I was and whom I had thought I became. I was afraid of everyone all the adults. If only I was born as a boy and not a girl or maybe if I were not born at all, maybe I wouldn't have these things done to me. I could handle the beatings, as the beatings continued, the stronger I was getting. At nine years old, my height was 4'10" weighting 100 lbs. my father was in the 5' 6" area and weighing approximately 260 lbs. I am just guessing, because I can't remember.

Now things are getting bad, I knew I am trapped and not able to do anything about it, the abuse kept getting worse. There was this one time he was home alone with me. Mom was gone to the hairdresser. He made me come up to their bedroom, and made me lay on the bed, he went over to his dresser and put something on his hands, and came over and rubbed it on my crotch. It burned, I began to cry and scream. He jumped on top of me, held me down with his hand over my mouth and nose, I couldn't breathe, and he was so heavy. I thought I was on fire it was burning so much. He said; this will clean your dirty little snatch, it is my cologne, it has alcohol in it and will kill all the germs. It will stop in a minute, the burning you feel is all the germs you have down there, be thankful it's not rubbing alcohol, I'm using.

On Tuesday nights, he would want to go to the sales barn and would demand for me to go along, even though mom said, it's a school night, she needs to go to bed early. He told her, she likes to see the animals, and one night won't hurt her and it's not on during the day, or weekends. We would never make it there. He would go down a dark side road and stop the car. I never knew that there where so many things a man could do to a child or person. He penetrated me the first time. I screamed and started to cry, it hurt. He put his hand over my mouth, yelling at me stop crying and screaming. It will not help any; no one will hear you. His hands were so big they covered my nose, I could not breathe, and nothing I could do. He continued, and said, you are nothing but a dirty little Indian as he is doing his thing, and after he was finished I asked, why do you call me a little Indian and why do you do this to me? His reply;" because that is what you are, you were born to an Indian, and all Indians are alike, only good for sex". "They have no brains. They cannot do anything for themselves, and that is what you are, and last, because I can and no one will believe you" with a big grin on his face.

When I went home, he told my mother that I went number 1 in my pants, and that is why he gave me the strap. It really wasn't Pee that was in my pants it was from him. My mother did not look she took my father's word for it.

My mother was a wonderful woman; she did not show much affection and had not much knowledge, she told me she only had Grade four schooling. She was almost like a robot and did what her master told. She never wanted any one to hug her; she didn't like that. One day I asked my mom. Why did you adopt me? Her reply was, "I didn't want you or to adopt you, and I didn't want to love you, because I knew what was going to happen, referring to the beatings and I could not stop it she replied. I hadn't told her what my dad was doing to me, yet I wasn't sure she would believe me any ways. I said, how did you know what was going to happen. Well, your dad beat your brother so bad he was black and blue for a long time, from his shoulders down to the bottom of his butt. Just because he cried when he was sick, from the pneumonia he had and your dad wanted him to have his picture taken and stop crying. He was just learning to sit up, and then it took a long time for him to sit up again.

The next Tuesday, He was going to take me to the sales barn again. I had told mom I did not want to go, but I did not tell her the reason why I didn't want to go, I thought she wouldn't believe me anyway. She told dad that she wanted me at home to do some work around the house to help her. He got so mad he screamed at mom. She is my daughter too, Mom said, well then I will go too, that only made him madder **"NO"** He screams, you stay here where you belong, mom said, if she goes, I go. He went in a rage, started swinging his arms, screaming, I do what I want. You are not going with us. You cannot tell me what I can and cannot do. She is going to come with me, and that is that. Mom asked; why don't you take your son? You never take him very much. I interrupted and said, Mom, It's OK, I will go. I cannot allow this to go on. It was upsetting to me and to my mom. I was in fear of our safety. (I felt) I was the cause of the argument. If I had never said, I did not want to go, it would not have happened, I knew what was in store for me. It was easier to go through, than to listen to him in a rage, and possibly hurt us. I knew if he continued his fist would start flying. I did not want that to happen. My father was supposed to be a good Christian man, we went to church twice every Sunday, and on Thursdays it was prayer meeting night. Sometimes we went on a Wednesday night too. I can't remember what it was about; there was a Young People's night that might have been on Wednesday night. It was another thing I couldn't go to, but my brother was allowed to.

The community looked up to my father; he would occasionally fill in for the ministers, when they were on holidays or sick. He could preach a good sermon; he was also involved with the barbershop quartet and sang at many church services. Therefore, when we made a noise that he did not like in church, we would get the strap in the bathroom of the church, just as we would at home. He had to show that discipline was give to his children to the code of the bible. Also made to do what they were told, not like many of the other children laughing and running around like little hoodlums, as he would call them, his famous saying was, Spare the rod; spoil the child, this was not only said by my father, but many others believed in it as well, and believe me they didn't spare the rod.

Prayers That My Father Would Die And Go To Hell

My father was at a rehearsal with the quartet, at the church and had a heart attack. I have to admit I was praying that day, that he would not make it through, that he would die and go to hell, but it didn't happen, he pulled through, what a disappointment that was, now I have to continue on with the verbal, physical, mental, and sexual abuse. Answering my prayers didn't happen. I felt alone, misunderstood and my willingness to live was not there.

The whole church was praying for him, and many others. It didn't seem like any one was praying for the ones who'd need the prayers, from his abuse. We had many people coming around giving their condolences and asking if they could help, but when we needed help, not many were available to.

When my father was in the hospital with his heart attack, I had to and wanted to, help my mother. We had to milk the cows, mom never knew how to milk a cow, and with the other chores, feeding the chickens, and go back in the forest on the tractor with a trailer and retrieve the year old wood for the stove, because my brother would not help. I really don't blame him for not helping because, he was physically, and mentally abused as well. I cannot say if anything else happened to him, but it is not my place to reveal his past. He has to reveal; what ever happened to him in order to heal himself, no one can do this for him. He didn't know what was happening to me and said you don't know what it's like, you've had it easy; I have never forgotten what he had said that day.

We had no wood for the stove to keep us warm and my mother did not know how to drive. So I said to her, I can drive the tractor, dad taught me how to drive and change gears, she said, OK, but I'm coming with you don't go too fast. I replied, no, I would go slowly. So we went to the bush to get the wood, we filled up the trailer with wood and came back home, and we piled it into the wood-shed. Splitting the wood was all we had left to do. I said to mom, I can do that too, she said, you're too little, you will likely cut your foot off, no I won't, I can split it and not hurt myself. I started to split the wood and a smile came over her face, you're quite strong for your size, and I smiled. I need to become strong, so I could defend myself because; it was life and death for me when he comes home. I knew I had to be strong, physically and mentally, in order, to fight against him, and win.

My father also taught me how to kill a chicken, so when mom needed to have the chicken killed for dinner, she went out and tried to do it, but she had no strength. She felt sorry for the chicken and couldn't do it, so I was there and told her I would do it. I did, she was shocked that I knew and could do it without any feeling. Dad taught me very well on how to kill. Mom turned to me and asked me, how you can do that without crying or any feeling, why have you become a very cold-hearted person? I never taught you that, my reply was, it's only a chicken, and then I told her all the stuff dad had taught me about killing things. She didn't know what to say. You could see in her face that she was frightened; this is when she told me, someone from the church had told her I was possessed with a demon. I started to laugh, no I'm not, she said, it is beginning to look like you are, you don't have any feelings any more at least you don't show them, why should I show feelings when I get beat all the time for having them? You know yourself, if we do anything make a noise, say anything at dinner table, we get a backhander from dad and his words are kids are to be seen and not heard, You know that yourself, there is nothing that we can do right, to please dad. We can't even play outside without dad coming up screaming and hitting us for no reason.

He was feeling good when they released from the hospital, and he came home, he seemed to be a better man, nicer that is, but it didn't take long for him to get back to the same way he used to be. When he started back to work, I asked my mother, if I could go up on the hill and have a picnic by myself, She said yes, Only if you hear the whistle blow, you must come back in a hurry because your dad is due home, and you know what will happen if you are not here. I agreed. She packed me a lunch with sandwiches that had more than one item. My father forbid us to have butter and cheese, we were only allowed one or the other and pickles, which was great because I was not allowed a lot of pickles. I headed for the Hill, and this was a large hill. It took me approximately 15 minutes to get to the top. I felt like I was on top of the world and closer to God. That is why I wanted to go, so I could talk to God, one-on-one. I sat down and started to talk to God, before I ate my lunch. I said, God, why do you allow him to do this to me. Are you real, why was I born? Everyone says, you will talk to them and that I could hear you if I talked to you. Why can I not hear you now, and am I that bad of a kid and don't know it? Have I made you mad at me? Do all fathers do this to their children? Why do we have to live like this? What is the purpose of living? Can you answer any of these? If no one wants me here on earth, can you take me there? If you don't want me, does that mean, I will go to hell? I really don't want to be here. I don't want to live on this earth, if I have to do this all my life. It does not make any sense to me. I sat and ate my lunch and enjoy the peaceful surroundings, the rabbits, and squirrels. I looked at the trees and the flowers with the bees flying around, the blue sky with the white clouds and said did you really make all the nice things I am looking at. I do not understand how you could be so nice, and yet not help anyone that is in trouble. Just in case you are busy and can't get back to me right now, I can understand. I will wait to hear from you, please answer me, as soon as you can. Thank you

He never answered me that day, in words that you can hear that it is. It took a lot of years for me to figure out that it is a feeling not a voice you hear, and in your heart that you hear God's voice.

All of a sudden, the whistle blew, and I knew my dad was almost home. I was running, falling down the hill trying to get home as fast as possible, and I made it, he did not know I was up there by myself, on the Hill, it was close. I smiled at mom, and she smiled back, she was not going to tell dad, it was our secret. That day I wrote this poem.

Darkness and the light

Darkness, no one can see me.
No one can tell what happens in the darkness, it is a secret.
Not ever to be told
I feel the hands over me in the darkness.
Stay in the darkness, I am safe.
No one can see me in darkness.

I hear the voices of children playing in the light
I hear their laughter. They are not in the darkness.
Why can I not go into the light? It is safer in the darkness.
Bad things happen in the darkness. There is pain in the darkness
I hear screams and sounds of terror.
Coming from me only in the darkness

A hand reaches in to the darkness. Come out in the light.
I cannot, you do not know me. Someone will hurt me in the light.
The Darkness is better no one can see me or hear me

I yell into the light, please help me, but no one can see me or hear
me. Then, I hear a voice, come out into the light again
No, I cannot, you will hate me, and I am bad, I am deformed
and ugly with no mind of my own.
I must stay in the dark, for I am evil and not for the light.

I am lost in the dark at the point of no return. I clench my cheeks
with my teeth, until Blood is running. Therefore, no one can hear
me cry, inside the darkness. I cannot see the light, only darkness.
This is where I will stay, but I want to go into the light.
I cannot, they will hurt me. They will know I am from darkness,
and not the light. My life will end if I go into the light.
They do not understand because they are in the light.
There is sunshine, but it is still darkness for me.

It Was Time To Try To Do Something.
But Sickness Set In

I began getting pains in my right side, every time I would run. Mom took me to the doctor and the doctor said, he didn't think it was too serious right now, and not to worry about it, there is a possibility it could be her appendix, but of course, my dad, thought I was faking. This went on for a year, finally, the doctor said, we have to check this out, and he sent me to a specialist. I had a lot of tests done, while they were doing a test, I threw up, my temperature was elevated, and he immediately set up for surgery in a couple hours and told my parents my appendix were about to bust, and needed emergency surgery. My father could not believe this and said to my mother, she convinced him to do this; all she wants is attention. When the operation was finished, the nurse was a friend of my mother and told her what I had said, while I was sleeping, that I did not want to live, and I was going to kill myself. Mom never told me what the nurse had said.

After thinking for a long time, I decided I would not live on this earth; it was time for me to leave, so over a six-month period, I started stealing my father's sleeping pills. I would only take two out of the bottle at a time, so he would not know they were gone. At the end of the six months, I went to school and took the pills in class, when one of the kids saw me, I ran out of the classroom, and she told the teacher. All I remember after taking the pills was the vice principal, walking me up, and down the hall and making me drink water. That is all I remember and telling him, I do not want to live any more, just let me die. I remember him saying, why don't you not want to live anymore? My reply was, I just don't, I wasn't about to tell him what was going on.

I woke up later that day in the children's ward with my hands tied to the bedrails and IV in both arms. I was angry and mad that I was alive, and being a strong child, I ripped both arms out of the restraints, and then took the IV out of my arms. Nurses came running, it took three nurses to hold me down, and I really did not want to live. There was a nurse that stayed by my side, until I had settled down, then I asked her, can you call my teacher to come visit me, I was crying and said, I would really like to talk to her. The nurse said she would try but could not promise anything, the same nurse asked me, why did you try to take your life, I told her, my father was doing things to me and I did not want to live anymore, but I never told her what he was doing to me.

The nurse came in and said you have a visitor; I started to feel frightened, thinking it was my parents coming, but to my surprise, it was my teacher. I was happy, I told her, some things I can't remember what or if it was the secrets that I was holding, but she made me feel like a person. She is very special to my heart, even to this day. She settled me down and I felt at ease. She brought me some things like hand cream, and some other things. This was foreign to me. She didn't have to come visit me in the hospital, but she did, I wanted her to know that I wasn't trying to kill myself because of her, I was doing it because of my father. I thought she might be upset at me when I took the pills in her class. I didn't think of this before I took the pills, that it would hurt other people that I did not want hurt.

The next day, my parents came to visit. They were refused entry into my room, I don't know why, unless they were investigating what I had said. I had asked the nurses not to allow my father to come in. I was truly frightened of the outcome, I was alive, and I did not expect to be. This made things much worse, because they sent me right back into the abuse. Children services didn't even get involved. When I started back to school after coming out of the hospital, the school requested an assessment on me.

I am in receipt of your letter Dated October 4th, 2004, requesting file information pertaining to Deborah Duffield D.O.B. November 7, 1955. I have confirmed Ms Duffield came into the care in November 1958, and was later adopted by the family in 1960. Our file history related to Ms Duffield's birth family and a brief adoption file, which consists of home visits and reference to Deborah experiencing earache problems that eventually resulted in a tonsillectomy on March 19, 1959.

Enclosed is a report dated June 2, 1967 from the Clinic that appears to be a Binet Intelligence Test of Deborah. The psychologist, identified Deborah as having a Childhood Behavior Disorder. The document was found in our microfilmed files but unfortunately, there is no reference to the origin or purpose.

Our records do not contain evidence indicating Deborah returned to the care as a child " found in need of protection " after her adoption. There is also no record of abuse of Deborah by her adoptive parents.

This report has been retyped because the original was not able to seen after scanning it.

Name:	Debbie
Chronological age:	11.6 years
Mental age:	9.10 years
I.Q.:	(86) 81 - 91

Psychological interview revealed a white, female, eleven-and-a half-year-old patient of satisfactory physical development. During the contact, she remained cooperative and spontaneous but displayed a very noticeable defeatist outlook about her ability to meet the demands of the situation. She appeared to be very immature in her reasoning and thought processes. Her intellectual resources indicated by or test results, place her at a slight academic disadvantage. She should, however, be capable of completing grade four requirements. We believe that her lack of self-esteem may have adversely influenced her intelligence test result. She is probably endowed with ability at the lower end of the normal range.

Our impression of this girl is that her attitude is a reflection of home conditioning. She has not been entirely successful in building a wholesome attitude towards herself and her capabilities. She lacks self-confidence and does not have a clear sense of identity. She has not achieved emotional independence from her parents and has little maturity and sense of responsibility for girl of her age. She will need help in developing a more positive outlook about herself and her abilities in learning to make choices and take responsibilities.

We feel that her parents have done a great deal to undermine her confidence by their anticipant attitude of failure with regard to her and ambitions, and the achievement's. She should be encouraged to do things at which she can succeed and should be commended for her efforts and "good tries". She should be invited to join freely in-group activities, and when she fails, she can rally to try again.

It would be advisable for the parents to be made aware of our impressions in order that they might adopt a more realistic and less protective and pessimistic attitude towards their daughter's potential abilities.

Diagnosis: Childhood Behaviour Disorder

Psychologist

This report was ignored and used against me, because my father never read it properly or maybe he did, but just didn't tell my mother the truth of what it said, because she had a problem reading.

They sent me to a psychiatrist. It took the psychiatrist a long time to get me to talk. He told me he would not tell my father, what I said, and promised. Eventually, I told him what my father was doing, but not the whole story, and the session ended, then he asked my father to come in, and my father was in there a long time. I was afraid that he, the psychiatrist, was telling him, my father, what I had told him and I was right, he did tell. My father came out to the truck and said, he told me what you told him. He does not believe you, I told him, it was an outright lie, and he said, for me to kick you in the ass and give you a licking within an inch of your life for telling such a lie. We never made it home that day after the meeting, I don't have to say what happened, you already know.

My father said, you don't know anything, you can't look after yourself, you even tried to commit suicide, you proved that you are not capable to learn or to do anything. I am going to talk to your mother about putting you into a mental institution, where I don't have to worry about you no more and telling everyone what I'm doing to you, you know they won't believe you, I've proven to everyone that you're making it all up, it's for your own good. I said why are you doing this, why are you lying, you tell me it is not right to lie, but you lie. I have never done anything to you, but I am going to start.

This is when I gave up, totally, the will to live, honesty, kindness and my behaviour, because I could not talk right, read right, eat properly, walk properly, wiping myself after going to the bathroom wasn't good enough, I used too much toilet paper and didn't fold it right either, also he even said I couldn't breathe right, that I breathed too loud, and I chewed too loud, people should not hear me chewing, there was nothing, absolutely nothing that I did right, even to buttering bread or doing dishes, one little mark on any dish, even if I didn't do that dish, everything in all the cupboards would be in the sink for me to do over, and it had to be really hot water not lukewarm were I could handle them, my hands were red from the almost boiling water. I was a freak, not human, a disgrace to the world.

Washing my hair, on a Sunday was a sin. If I was caught, there was a big fight with my father, I would be beaten with the fist, not the strap, thrown against walls, or the wood stove and choked. The older I got the more I would fight back. My mother would often be crying, because my father would come after one of us. Sometimes for no reason or his reasons did not make any sense. I will tell you this part because it affected me as much as my brother

Dad gave my brother a calf to look after, and feed it until it was big enough for selling and he could keep the profit that he would make. He named it Brownie, because it was brown. My brother was so proud of the calf. We came home from school and sat down for supper. My brother asked where's Brownie, I didn't see him out in the barn yard, my father's reply was; you're eating him, and started to laugh and thought it was really funny, He had taken the calf to slaughter and didn't tell my brother. My brother could not eat and left the table and all the while you could see my brother was hurt, but he did not cry, because he knew what would happen if he did. My mother said, why did you have to say it at suppertime, you could have waited. He has to learn some time, and it might as well be now. The calves are not raised to be pets, they are for food. That is not the only time my father did things to hurt, my brother, but I will not get in to what happened with my brother.

My Hands & Feet Were Frozen Not Just Cold

One day my Dad brought home a new snowmobile, and my brother and he went out on it, they seemed to have a lot of fun on the snowmobile until my brother did something to it that my father did not like, but he still was able to ride on it. I don't know what my father did to him for breaking the snowmobile. My father believed in dividing and conquering so neither, one of us knew what was happening to the other, unless it was a fluke.

It came the day when mom and dad bought me a brand new snowsuit, all one piece. I was so proud of myself in my new snowsuit and thought it would be good to have, so I would be safe to go snowmobile with my father. It wasn't a snowmobile suit, but it was still warm. When we took off, it was daylight. I was having fun; I couldn't believe it riding on the back bouncing up and down from the snow drifts being so high. I really believed he wasn't going to be able to do anything to me because it was so hard to get my snowsuit off and on, but I was wrong again. Darkness set in and the fun turned into fear. He stops the snowmobile there was nothing but silence and darkness. I don't know where we were. He said he had to go to the bathroom. That didn't seem too strange, but when he came back, he began to undo my snowsuit and told me to go to the bathroom as it would be a long way back, so I went to bathroom. Then he would not let me put my snowsuit back on, but took my pants off too, I was cold, and it was snowing. I had no boots, hat, mitts, snowsuit, or pants on. I was freezing and started to shake, being so cold, he wouldn't stop. I said in a shaky voice please don't do this, please. He said shut up you little slut. This is when he started doing it up my buttocks, he said, I am doing this so I don't get you pregnant and, I don't give a damn, if you freeze or not, you don't want to live, anyways. You already tried to kill yourself and you couldn't even do that right, that shows how stupid you are, I did not do anything or say anything, because my hands and feet were froze, they hurt so bad I couldn't walk, by the time my dad finished and put my boots back on, they had snow in them. My mitts and snowsuit where full of snow, and he put them on anyway, not knocking the snow out, I could hardly hold on while we headed home, the snowsuit was frozen to me in the cold wind, no helmet or scarf and on the back of the snowmobile. When I hobbled in the door I fell to my knees, my mother rushed over to me and asked, why are you all ice, let's get this stuff all off you and over by the wood stove to warm up and dry you off. Dad! She yelled, She is covered in ice, wet, and frozen to the bone, her hands, and feet are solid white, I think she is frostbitten why is she like this? He responded well she had go to the bathroom, so she took off her snowsuit and boots it is a one-piece snowsuit. She couldn't do much else, if she wanted to go to the bathroom, could she? Next year, we will buy her a two-piece snowsuit. She will be fine a little cold will not hurt her; it is not as bad as she is making it out to be.

The next day my father took me out to the barn. I thought he was going to do the same thing again, but he didn't. He said Dub we need to have a talk. If you stop telling everyone, I will put it in my will that you get the farm. (It was a 300-acre farm) My response, I do not want your farm, or money. I don't want any part of it or you. I'm not going to call you my father or dad anymore, either. You have told me because I am adopted and not your blood that I am not your daughter, and that is why you can do things to me and not call it incest, so I figure, you're not my father either. I will be calling you sir or Mr. *** but not dad. It is going to come to a point here, where you are going to kill me or I am going to kill you, and I will not regret it if I do, and I will be much happier if you kill me then you will go to jail. He said they will not send me to jail, you little fool, all I have to say is you tried to kill me like all the other times, and all will be forgotten. I said; I am not going to keep on living like this, life is not worth living, so keep your stupid farm, and everything else, I don't want it. You think that I am dumb enough that you're going to give me the farm when you die, just so you can do this me now. I am sorry, I'm a little smarter than you think, you have no intentions of ever giving me anything, you're just saying that so you can continue doing what you want to me and proving to yourself how dumb you think I am. He said, you have tried everything you can so far, and no one believes you, what makes you think people are going to believe you now? I told him, you are going to make a mistake, one of these days, and that is when they will believe me. I said, by the way, what happened to my quarter mom gave me, and I asked you to hold on to it, until I got downstairs, from getting dressed, to go to town with mom, and you denied

I even gave it to you? I kept it, he replied, to teach you a lesson, for you not to trust anyone, not even me, so you will remember that people in your life are not to be trusted ever. If you want to survive in this world, you will not trust anyone, not even yourself, and always question what you do, more than likely you're wrong.

When I Wanted To Kill Him

One-time you showed me, what you and your six army friends did to a girl, because she was asking for it, (the girl was in the army as well, and dad called her a whack) Are you saying I'm asking for it? He said; yes, you are, all women ask for it, it is just their nature. I asked, did you always do this stuff to girls, he said, yes, that's what girls and women are for, then I said, did you ever get caught doing things to women? His response; if I was caught I would not be here; I know what I am doing, in a rough voice, that is why I am a man and you are a woman. Women, think they know everything, but they don't, they haven't got a clue.

I went back over to the house and told mom that I would not be calling him dad anymore, and she asked me why I said; I don't like him, I don't want him as my father and he said I'm not his daughter, because I am not his flesh and blood. She said by the law, he is your father, and the court said so, when we adopted you. I didn't ask to be adopted or born or go through what I'm going through, so I don't care what the court said, I'm not going to call him my father. As far as I am concerned, he is not my father. She started to cry, and said, that means I am not your mother either then, my reply; yes, you are my mother, but he is not my father and from that day on, I never called him dad. For a couple of years, this went on, where I called him Mr. ** or Sir, and my mother came to me and said, if you don't start calling him dad, don't call me mom anymore. I did not want to hurt my mom, so I gave in and called him dad, but most of the time, I avoided him, so I would not have called him anything. There were plenty of things I wanted to call him, but I couldn't at that time.

I tried to kill him a couple of times, and a friend of mine at school knew and went to counsellor and told them what I was planning to do that day. The counsellor kept their eyes open, and as they saw me running down the hall way toward him,(my father,) with his hunting knife in my hand, someone pulled me into a room, it was one of counsellors, they said, you don't want to do this, you will go to jail for murder. I said I didn't care, it would be better than the way I am living now.

Another time, I tried was when mom and dad went grocery shopping, and I was left all alone at the house, this gave me the perfect opportunity to find his gun and kill him, I was going through everything frantically, trying to find the handgun, and the bullets. I sat down to think, where would he keep the key to the gun rack I needed to get the key, I couldn't find it so, I picked the lock, and there was the gun, but no bullets, I couldn't find the bullets. Then I heard them drive in the driveway. I hurried to put the gun back and relock the gun rack. He never knew what I was planning on doing, if I had succeeded, he would have died that day. Then I was thinking, he has a pen gun, if I could find that, but I never did find it, he had that hid because it was illegal.

Things That Started Happening With My Grandmother and Mother

My grandmother was a wonderful woman and my mother confided in her many times, Grandma was very smart, at least I think so. It was on the weekend. When we sat down for dinner, as usual, dad would pull out the Bible and read from what ever he thought should be read that day, my brother and dad would have a discussion on their views on what he read but an argument broke out, they were yelling at each other. My mother started choking. We tried to help but what ever was stuck wouldn't come up and it wouldn't go down. There was enough room for air to go through, so Dad call the Dr. When the doctor came he checked my mom out, he made her lie down on the couch and gave her a needle and said, her nerves had closed her throat off and that she will have to take it easy, from now on. This happened many times; of course, my father would never listen to anyone, not even the doctor. One time, the doctor did everything he could and said I'm not sure it's going to work this time, we will have to wait and see, it went on for a long-time, but she finally came around. I was very happy; I would have liked it to be dad, which would have suited me just fine. He didn't care about anyone only himself. He said, mom. You have to calm down and quit getting so upset, all I am doing is discussing the Bible, and getting upset will not help.

Grandma fasted for days, and prayed, after this incident with mom. She was a very religious woman and believed in God, to her dying day. She felt that fasting would help save her son from all the evil that he was doing, and his thoughts, but that didn't help dad. I don't think anything could've helped him; he was pure evil. It seemed like Grandma was always fasting, for some reason or another. One day we're sitting at the kitchen table having our supper. Dad brought out the Bible and began to read, just then, Grandma started to mumble. We thought she was praying to herself, so we all continued to read the Bible and prayed. When we were all done, I said, Grandma, are you okay, there was no response, she continued, mumbling sitting there rocking back and forth with tears running down her cheeks. Dads said, leave her alone, she is praying. I knew there was something wrong, grandma would always grab my hand and say everything was OK, and I would go along with what ever I was doing, this time was different. She never made any movement only rocking back and forth and crying. Mom came over to Grandma and tried to get a response and even she couldn't, she said, dad there is something wrong. He came over and couldn't get Grandma to do anything either, they called the Doctor, when he came, he said that Grandma has had a stroke, they took her to the hospital. I was so sad that day; Grandma never recognized me or talked to me after that day.

Dad started yelling at me saying it was my fault that Grandma had a stroke, because I told her what he was doing to me, and if she hadn't been told she wouldn't have been fasting and none of this would've happened. I was holding back the anger, thinking he is right. I shouldn't have told and she would've been fine.

Finally, after a couple of weeks, grandma came home. She wasn't the same; she didn't know anyone. She always talked about old times, when we were younger.

He continued telling me it was my fault, but mom never said a word, so, I believed it. I did everything I could to help Grandma when she came home; I bathed her, fed her, changed her, lifted her into the rocking chair, and did many things. I felt so guilty if I only had kept my mouth shut, she wouldn't be this way. Eventually, my dad put her in a nursing home and I would never see her again until I left home. Grandma was gone so they turned her room in to a study. Dad decided to buy a puppy for mom; it was a teacup poodle. She was so cute. It didn't take long, for dad to hurt the little thing, she ended up with two broken back legs, but moms said it was an accident. I never believed it.

Dad decided to breed the poodle and have puppies; they were going to sell them. I ended up watching all night to make sure the puppies, never whined, because one time, a puppy whined and dad killed it, I didn't want to see the puppies murdered so I slept on the La-Z-Boy chair, by the puppies' door.

My first year of high school was very disturbing and upsetting. All the students had to go three days a week because we were sharing a school until our new high school was built. It was confusing for all the students on both sides. The days I had to go to school my father would drive me and pick me up after school, because he was afraid that I might get into trouble. I was in special education for the students that can't learn, the teacher decided to have us try Chinese green tea. She packed each student an envelope containing enough for two or three cups and sealed it. I put mine in my backpack to try when I got home. I forgot that it was in my backpack and my dad went through it and found it. He didn't ask me what it was he just called the police the OPP. I got up to go to school and he told me I wouldn't be going to school for a while, I ask why; because of the drugs you had in your backpack, that stuff you call marijuana. I told him I didn't have any marijuana and I don't understand what you're talking about. He said, you lie all the time the police have the package and there going to test it and when they do you're going to jail. I only had Chinese green tea; the teacher gave it to all of us in my backpack I replied. You won't fool the police department, when they tested and find out it is marijuana you are going to go to jail and don't expect me or your mother to bail you out, it's won't happen. I was out of school for six months, and I asked my mother will I ever be able to go back to school, she replied as soon as the police get back to us and let us know what is happening you probably will be able to go back to school. I ask her when are they supposed to call she replied I don't know your dad is looking after that, I said asked dad to call the Police and find out what's happening, because it is only Chinese tea, she said OK. It took my father several days, but then he had the answer, your daughter is awful stupid for buying Chinese tea thinking it was marijuana, that was their reply. I started back to school but I was already six months behind everyone else and knew I could never catch up. I ended up doing my grade nine all over again.

Shortly after, mom started getting sick, they found out she had cancer of bowel, also known colon cancer and this also was blamed on me, dad said it was my fault because I got mom upset over Grandma, and I always had her upset over every thing, I was a bad kid. He said anyone that is around me for any length of time is going to die, because I am so evil. That hurt me so bad, I wanted to die right there on the spot, so I went and found some pills, and took them. I didn't know if there were enough for an overdose or not, all I wanted was to be nonexistent, I guess you could say I tried killing myself then, but I lived, and no one knew that I had taken the pills. No one seemed to care if I lived or died that's why I didn't want to live.

Everything around me wasn't real anymore. I didn't know where to turn, where to go, because if mom went in the hospital, that meant my father would be happy because I'm left with him, so he could do what he wanted, there was nothing I could do to stop it from happening, short of killing myself or running away. Mom went in for all sorts of tests and they said surgery is her only option. Mom went in for her surgery, and I cannot remember being at home or her having the surgery or any of that space in time. I must have blocked that part out because I do not remember. I do remember when she came home, how sick she was. I did everything I could for her to make sure she was comfortable. It wasn't too long after she was well enough that I left home. I went to school, and never came back.

I Left Their House Forever
It Was Never My Home

There was a program at school for students to go out and learn what work was like and to get some experience. My father did not like me going to this, but he could not say a thing, because the school required it. That gave me the perfect opportunity to get away, but then it was like jumping from the frying pan in to the fire. I met this man, while I was on my co-op at the hospital kitchen. He was nice, and we became friends. I told him a little bit, about what was happening at home. (What a mistake). He told me I didn't have to live like that, and he would help me get out of there. I was excited, now I could leave my parent's house. He said I could stay at his house; he even bought me a ring and said he loved me. That was nice; no one had told me that before, I thought I was in love. He never touched me sexually, or even asked. He was a prince to me. I asked him how old he was. He said thirty-two I was only 15 but that never made a difference to me. I believed that age never did matter as long as you were good to each other, and loved each other,

(but what did I know about love there wasn't any in the family home and he lied he was much older than 32 but I didn't know at that time.)

My parent's knew I was drawn to this man and my mind was set to be with him, no matter what the cost. I believed because he was so nice to me, we were meant to be together, he never hit me, yelled at me, or any of what had happened at home. He was a perfect gentleman, and I believed I deserved that in my life. Anything would have been better than living at home with my parents. A home that I felt was not mine. I went to school, then to my co-op work program, that is when I decided not to go home, and I stayed with this man, that I called boyfriend at that time. I stayed hidden, so my father would never be able to find me, because if he had he would have beaten or killed me.

I phoned my mother, the next day and she was crying, uncontrollably I told her; I had to leave, because of my father. I could not take it any longer, and she agreed. She asked me if I could phone her, when dad was not there. I told her I would, and that I loved her. Just because I left, that didn't mean I would never be able to talk to her again.

Shortly after I left home, my mother's cancer came back, and they needed to operate. She went in to hospital and had this surgery called colostomy. They put her in intensive care. She was very sick. I went up to the hospital to see her, and as everybody knows, you have to buzz to get in to see anyone in intensive care and you have to be related to get in. Well dad was there; he came out and said your mother doesn't love you, she wants nothing to do with you so, you just go and do whatever you do and get out of here. I was heartbroken, I love my mother very much, and I knew she didn't say that. I left and came back. Shortly after I saw my father leave, I went up to intensive care and buzzed them let me in and nurse came to the door, and said your father has left strict instructions not to allow you in, I started to cry, and said in a crackled voice, ask my mother and if she says that I will leave, still crying uncontrollably having a hard time catching my breath. She came back to the door and said your mother wants to see you, which made me cry even harder. I was having a hard time to talk but I ask Mom did you say that you don't love me? She was crying and said no, that is your father saying that, not me. The nurses came over and tried to help us calm down, because it was hard on mom just having surgery. I told mom I love you and I will be back, but I would make sure Dad wasn't around, she smiled and the nurse gave her a needle so she could sleep and I left feeling better and the hatred toward my father was building even more, man I hate him.

The next day I went up to see mom. Dad hadn't come up yet, so we had a good talk, then the buzzer went off, we thought we had been caught, one of the nurses came over while the other one went to the door, she grabbed my arm and took me out the back way and he didn't even no I was there. I was so scared that he was going to take it out on mom, but mom said the next day that the nurses told dad they hadn't seen me and mom was so happy. It is a terrible life to hide all the time.

I went to my boyfriend's place. Was telling him all the things that had happened in the last couple of days, he said; that guy needs to be shot and peed on, I started to laugh and he said, I am serious I will do it for you, all you have to do is say so and it will be done. Wow, I don't want to have any one else doing it, I want to deal with this myself, it is my family and my decision not yours or anyone else for that matter, so don't be saying that or telling any one what I said to you.

My mom finally got out of the hospital and was doing well. I phoned mom, and asked if I could come over to the house. Maybe I could take her out for dinner, she said yes your dad is at work and she had to be home before him. I told her that I would have her back home so he wouldn't know, I picked her up and went into town to a Chinese restaurant and talked and had lunch. I asked mom, would you come live with me?, I will look after you and pay the bills and give you the money all you would have to do is look after the house work and then do what you want. She said no she couldn't do that, she loved my dad. I was REALLY mad and said; how can you love him when he treats you like shit. Abuses his kids, she said she had never been on her own and was afraid too. That is no reason to stay with him, I said he doesn't love you or any one else, then I told her what he had done to me and that he was going out with another woman when she was in hospital, but that did not make her change her mind. Mom just said that she couldn't and please don't talk about this any more and I said ok. Mom said she was afraid of something and wanted to tell me, so she told me, she was scared of someone trying to have sex where her colostomy is, and not where they normally have sex, I said what would make you think that would happen, mom. She said that she was afraid that dad would want to try it and she said if she said no that he might get mad at her, my answer was you need to leave him he is not a nice person, she started to cry I say mom PLEASE come with me, the answer was no she couldn't. It was time to take her back home and she said you know you're a good little driver, I am not scared like I am with your father, I smiled and said that's because I am me and not my father. We arrived back to mom's home, said our goodbyes and off I went. I was on my way back to where I was living, when everything mom and I talked about came up. I wanted to die, and not have to do or think any more, I thought of steering the car into the canal, to stepping on the gas and hitting a tree, I couldn't, I had to stay around for mom. I went to the bar where I knew I could drink, being under age, and I got totalled, so bad they took me to the hospital emerge with alcohol poisoning, I almost didn't make it through that time, but I did and stayed drinking for a long time. The only thing in my life that comforted me at this time was the alcohol.

It was so nice not getting yelled at, or hit. I started to like this new life, but I wanted to finish my schooling and my boyfriend thought that would be a great idea too. So I went to school and asked if I could come back that I was out of the house. I was devastated, they said no. I live in another area, which I needed to go in that area. I said, please let me finish here I only have two months to go and school will be out for the summer, they said no, you have to go in the area you live, you more than likely will not get in until next year, most places won't start you this late in the school year. Well I went to the school they said and sure enough, they said not until next year so there went my schooling down the tubes. My boyfriend said don't worry you can go next year but that was too far ahead to foresee, because I didn't know if I could get a job with the grade I had. Grade 9, in two months it would have been my grade 10. What I didn't know was home economics isn't like real school. It was for sewing, cooking, hair dressing that kind of stuff not enough to get you a good job, just enough to function out in the world on your own. That wasn't enough to get a job. Everyone told me that I had to have grade 13 or I would be digging ditches for the rest of my life, and to back them up dad said I would never get one, because I was Indian, a woman and too dumb. I was going to show them, I am not as dumb as everyone thinks I am.

Here I go to my first job interview, all dressed in good clothes, and a smile. It was called manpower back then, the lady came out and said come with me, so I followed her; we came to an office where she said have a chair and sit down. She said what kind of work are you looking for? I said any she chuckled and said do you have a social insurance number? I smiled and responded what the heck is that, she started to laugh, and then she asks what grade I completed, being proud I said grade 9 & 9 months of 10. She couldn't stop laughing this was making me upset not knowing why she is laughing, but I said nothing and carried on with the interview. How old are you? Well I am 15 & 7 months, well she said go home you can't work you're too young, finish your schooling and get your sin number then come back and she walked me out.

Whom do I ask what a sin number is, without looking dumb? I phoned mom she answered the phone and I said mom don't laugh, what is a sin number? It is a social insurance number you need for working, well how do I get this thing? She said we have it here, and I will have to get your dad to get it out, he has the key to unlock the desk. My response was, he isn't going to give it to me, mom said I will talk with him and get it for you, I said ok.

A couple days went by before I called my mom to see if she had my Social Insurance card. She said your dad would not give it to you or me. He said you left and you won't be getting anything from here. You know his famous words; you made your own bed now lie in it, mom was crying she didn't know what to do, I said mom it is ok I know how to get it, just tell me when he is gone to work, I can do that, she said he leaves at 10 this morning, ok mom I am on my way and we hung up the phone. When I got there, mom said you are going to break it to get in. I said no not really, I know where he keeps the key. She said well I am going out to the woodshed and get some wood, ok I said. I knew that mom going to the woodshed was so she could honestly say she had seen nothing. The key was right where he always kept it and I went in and got my card and gave mom a big hug and kiss, I love you as I was heading out the door, talk to you later mom, have to get a job, so I don't have to depend on my boyfriend to support me.

The next day, I went out and found a job, but I had to lie about my age and schooling, that lie was eating me up so I quit after getting my week's pay and told them the truth, they thanked me for been truthful and rehired me with a raise, I was the happiest girl on the planet. The job was doing dishes in a restaurant, with a dishwasher even, not by hand, so cool.

I hadn't talked with mom for a while so I called and she was crying, mom what is wrong? Your dad said you can not come around or call anymore, that you're nothing but trouble that you have lied to me about working that you are one of those ladies of the night, you don't have a job in the restaurant, he said he had called and they never heard of you. Mom I am working there, he is lying; mom said I don't know who to believe anymore, you best stay away till he cools down. It was a long time before I called to see how mom was doing. I had left that job to do a better paying job, but I felt bad for leaving the restaurant they were so nice to me, they gave me their blessing and told me to go to the new job.

I started my new job. It was pumping gas and washing windshields, I loved it. My hours where from 6 am to 10 pm, but I had to hitch hike from the town I was living in to another, that took a lot of time, there were cabs and that cost me $20.00 a day, if I did that, it would have cost me $100.00 bucks a week and I couldn't afford that. This job was good and I loved it so much I even started to work

Saturdays too; it made me forget what was bothering me, so I thought.

My boyfriend started his B.S. he quit his job and started drinking all the time going to the bars and paying for all his friends' drinks, even if they were just strangers he would buy their drinks, food, give them money and also give things out of the apartment to them. I asked him why are you doing this and he said well you're making more money than me so I don't need to work. I started yelling, that isn't what we agreed on. I will not do it this way. I had to listen to what I was told at home, but I will not in this relationship. As far as I am concerned it is a two way street, or we are not going to be together. You have to work and so do I, we are not married, and the money I make is my own not yours. You don't give me your money only your part of the rent and bills, the rest is yours. He starts yelling saying well I paid for you until you got on your feet now you can pay for me until I get on mine. What in the world are you talking about I said, you quit your job, I didn't I left home to get out of the B.S. I was in, and you know that. If I have to give you all the money I make then it is not worth me being in the relationship is it, do you want me to take all your money when you are working? He said no, I said well then smarten up; you are older than I am, and supposed to know this stuff, and get a job, and then we can get married, as you want too. He went back to his boss and asked for his job back, he started the next day. It made me feel a lot better, which maybe everything was going to turn out for the good.

I still hadn't called mom to see if everything was ok or not, and she never called me. One day this car pulls up to the pumps, I thought it look like my dad's but said to myself nay he wouldn't come here, because he has a gas pump on the farm. I went to the driver's window and sure enough, it was dad and mom. I had mixed feelings, one of happiness and the other of fear, why did they come here and how did they know that I was working here, the last time I talked to mom I was at the restaurant, the one dad had said he called and I didn't work there!. Mom started to cry, so I went around the car and opened the door, she came out and gave me a big hug. That was different mom never gave hugs first, I said I am happy to see you, what is the pleasure of your coming to see me? She said well your dad stopped buying the gas for the tank at the house, so we stopped here to get gas and you know the rest. Well, I ran around to dad's side, and asked if he wanted it filled, he said yes. We didn't talk any more then we had to. Mom got back in the car and said in front of dad that she would call me later at my home, I said you have to call late because I work till 10 pm and likely wouldn't get home till 11 or so, she asked me to call her, when I had time, I replied; ok I will. That day was a good day, mom would believe me now, she saw me at work, and dad couldn't lie and say it wasn't my job. Wow, this is a good day. When I arrived, home my property owner was at the door knocking, he was here for the rent. I said; well my boyfriend should be here, he's likely sleeping, come-on in and I open the door and there was my boyfriend, as I said sound asleep on the floor with puke all around him, he passed out drunk. The landlord started yelling at me "your already a month behind in your rent and this will make it two months, I will give you to the end of this week and then you have to get out". Now what do I do? I have given all the money to my boyfriend to pay the rent and buy groceries, but he spent every penny on booze with his friends at the bar and I don't get another pay for two weeks. When my boy friend woke up, I asked him what he was going to do about the rent. He said I'll get it, and I said how are you going to get something we don't have? Well I will have to ask my mother she will give it to me; oh, you have a mother now! I thought your mother was dead, that's what you told your boss a while ago you had to go to her funeral. I just said that to get the three days off and the weekend, she really didn't die, and she is in Sarnia, my boss knows she isn't well, that she has a heart condition and could die any time. I said; you will have to tell him the truth when she really does die, he won't believe you and you won't get off. His reply was, yes I will I have told him, must be 5 times now and he always forgets.

Well I might as well forget about this, he has an answer for all of it and who am I to say it is wrong anyway, his boss doesn't stop him from doing it either. He asked his mom and she wired it to him and he had to pay her back. I had not met or seen this woman yet; I would love to meet her she sounds like someone cool, well I didn't get to meet her for another year.

We lost the apartment anyway because he didn't pay the landlord when his mother sent the money, and he had a good job too working at the hospital as head chef in the kitchen plus my pay we brought in $600. - $800 dollars every two weeks, and he still spent it all and wouldn't let me keep it in the bank. He convinced me the banks were thieves and wouldn't give it back when we wanted it. Still I believed him, thinking it wasn't all that believable, but he was supposed to know more than me, he was a man, to make things worse I was just a girl and an Indian, two strikes against me.

Well I did it I got one in the town I had my job and I only rented it for me. It was in a private home just a room with kitchen and bathroom privileges. I was so happy I was on my own, with no one to answer to. I went to see him in the hospital and told him I had moved in this new place, thinking he would be happy for me, but I was wrong he got angry, saying he had done so much for me and I was leaving him with nothing, nowhere to live when he gets out of the hospital. I said what did you expect me to do, stay living in the car. He said, no but you could have got one for the two of us. I felt so bad after I saw him, I went out and rented him a one bedroom apartment, so he would have somewhere to go when he got out of the hospital. That was a big mistake. When he got out of the hospital, he came over to my place, and while I was at work. He told the landlady that I was a runaway and he was my father. He also informed her he was going to charge her for harbouring a juvenile, but if she let me out of my lease that he wouldn't have her charged. So when I came home that night, she kicked me out, I ask her why she said , you know why and you're just a little liar too, so get the hell out and don't come back, I said what about my deposit she said ask your dad he has it. Oh no! Did he come here, yes he did now you go back home where you belong. I was so shocked that my dad came and did that , I thought for sure I would have to go back home. I went to my boyfriends'; not knowing it was not my father, which got me kicked out of there. To tell him what had happened, he was so sympathetic to my tragedy he offered to take me in again to help me out, that made me feel a little more relaxed, at least I could still work, and maybe find another place where my father wouldn't find me.

That next week, I was fired from the gas station because my boy friend kept calling, coming over, calling head office and my boss's house. That was enough to make me lose my job, now I had no home or job I was dependent on him again. I got mad and phoned mom and ask why did dad come to my place and had me kicked out and why did he keep my deposit, he had no right, mom said dad didn't do that, I thought she was covering for him and I hung-up, because my boy friend didn't let on it was him. I didn't find out until a couple months later that he had every intention of keeping me in his grip, just the way my dad did.

He lost his job again, and then things just kept getting worse. We were driving along and he had fell asleep, I looked over at him, blood was coming out of his mouth, and down onto his chest he became deathly ill, and was put in the hospital for internal bleeding, surgery on his stomach, and he didn't recover from this for 3 months. When he got out of the hospital he fell and broke open his stitches and had to go back in for another month, and I had to live in the car until I could get enough money to get another apartment to live in. I lived in the car for 3 or 4 months in the winter I had to bath in the icy water, it was in January. I was hungry and had no money to buy food so I was going to steal it so I would go to jail, then I would have somewhere warm and some food. That didn't work, I went in the IDA store grabbed up an armful of anything and started to walk out the door, the girl stopped me and said is there anything else I can help you with and I said no and walked out the door, she didn't come after me at all, so I walked over to the police station and put it on the counter, the sergeant came over and said; Deb I know what your doing, now take it back, we are not going to put you in jail, we will call the salvation army and see if they can help, and they did for two nights. I was thankful for what I did get. Then I tried to get welfare and the woman said I didn't qualify, so that left me still in the car. The police officer that kept an eye on me came over to the car and said Deb try the welfare office they should help, I said I did, they can't help me I don't qualify, he replied come with me, we went down and tried again and the lady said NO, so the police man then went even higher up than her, to her boss he said yes and a check would be there next week, I was jumping for joy and gave the police man a big hug and said I will never forget what you have done for me, all I did was my job, he replied. No other police officers would have given me the time of day, I said. The next week came and she said there was no check for me, it never came, I started to think, if I could only be brave enough to kill myself, I wouldn't have to go through this any more. I was sure this was not how life was supposed to be. Day after day a struggle to stay alive, I didn't think it was worth it, the police officer came by and said; why aren't you out finding an apartment? Well that woman at the welfare office said; there isn't going to be a check for me, none came in, oh! He said; we will go and see her again. I was grinning from ear to ear. We got there and as I had told him, she said no, there isn't one and the police man stepped outside and phoned her boss. He said it was there he sent it himself, he came back in and asked her if she was absolutely sure there wasn't one in the desk, she replied; I said no and that means no, the police man turned his back and said I will not be responsible for what happens here, if you don't give her the check. She started to screaming , I am going to call the police, he said I am the police I cannot see anything wrong here, and I went over to her desk and tip it over and there came the check with my name on it floating through the air. She said I am going to make a report about this and you will be in trouble, the police officer turned around and said what happened to your desk, and help me put it back in place, we left and he said you take care and I haven't seen that policeman to this day. He was so nice and helped me when I couldn't do no more.

Married To A Man I Didn't Love In Addition, Moving To Another Country

I went out and got an apartment so when my boyfriend got out of the hospital he would have somewhere to live. I went up to the hospital to get him in a taxi and brought him home he had stitches all down his belly, and what they called spoons tied to these stitches. He was told he had to take care of himself and make sure he did not bust the stitches, but he didn't listen it was freezing rain out and he decided he wanted to go for a walk. Well he opened the door, we lived on the hill, I don't think his foot even landed on the first step, and down he went all the way to the bottom of the hill. The blood was gushing out all over the place, but all I could do was laugh, it did look awful funny to me. I called the ambulance and they took him back to the hospital. They said until you are better we are not releasing you. A couple of months down the road everything was back to normal if you want to call it normal.

We married so I wouldn't have to go back to live with my parents again. What I didn't know was he was married to two other women and only divorced from the second one, which didn't mean anything to the court system.

We moved to Kentucky. I thought things where bad in Canada, now I am in the United States and no way home, haven't got a clue which way is Canada either, and when I ask some one they said they didn't know, they even thought that United States owned Canada. I couldn't help but laugh at that statement. I am here so I might as well adapt and figure out what to do with my life. Things got even worse; my husband was going around saying I was his niece and he was looking after me, I knew then, that there was something going on. I talked to some of his friends and found out that he had a wife and 4 children in the next town and didn't want them to find out he married me. That was a shock. I confronted him, he told me that he did have kids there with another woman, but that was all, he had no feelings for the woman only the kids. I said; why have you been telling everyone that I am your niece and not your wife? His reply; they don't know what they're talking about; I never said any such thing. I didn't believe him now, there where too many lies I caught him in. I started working at a restaurant/gas bar. It was fun and we all got along, they teased me for having a Canadian accent, I had told them how I came there with my husband and wanted to go back, but needed to get some money and my licence so I could get back home. I came home from work exhausted from the restaurant, I went straight to bed, it didn't take me long to wake up. I had been bitten by a spider, I didn't know what kind, but a friend of ours down in the next trailer drove me to the hospital. She went back to find out if I had killed the spider in my sleep and I did she brought it back and it was a black widow. The hospital gave me two needles one in each hip of this pink stuff that looked almost like Pepto Bismol. I was in the hospital for two weeks. Now I am terrified of spiders. When they found out the trailer was infested with black widow spiders they decided to burn the trailer so it would not infest the rest of the park, there went my home. We moved into a two bedroom apartment for the rest of our stay there.

Things where going fine for the first while, until he bought the Kum Bak Tavern & Bar. I guess he thought that buying it would stop me from going back to Canada, and it worked for a while I was excited; I never owned something this nice before being only 18 and didn't know that you had to be 21 in a bar, I am moving up in the world now, so I thought. Boy, oh boy, what do I have myself into now?

My husband was in and out of the hospital so he could get the legal drugs and sympathy or attention, I didn't know which. Two state troopers came to the apartment. I was confused. They said; your husband sold the neon signs to the flea market. That is illegal; they belonged to the beer company, not to the tavern or us. I said; he could not have done that, he was in the hospital in Beaverdam; at least he was last night when I went there to visit him. They said; is this picture your husband? and showed me a picture and it was him, yes I said; that is him, we wouldn't arrest you if you get the signs back, there wasn't much else I could do, other than get them back and get the heck out of there. The thought of being arrested and in a jail of another country, Wow, it is so scary. I went to the people that sold the tavern to us and told them the whole story; they were so nice they helped me get the signs back so I wouldn't go to jail. They where happy to take the tavern back too, and resell it to people that wouldn't cause a problem like the one my husband did. They said it wasn't my fault but I felt it was.

I went to the Canadian Consulate and tried to see if they would deport me, but they said there was nothing they could do unless I was breaking the law, I wasn't breaking the law it was my husband. I went back to where my hubby was hiding, and said that I wasn't going to take this any more. I wanted to get a divorce, he just laughed at me and said where are you going to get the money to do that, because I'm not paying for it, and I will let you in on a little secret, that in Kentucky if the spouse didn't trust the other they had the right to kill them. Wow, I am in big trouble now, he can kill me if he wants to. There is nothing I can do about it. Why is it everyone wants to kill me, I must be the most terrible person on the earth. I have to get out of here and get back to Canada some how. I went to a friend for help, she told me how I could get back to Canada, to be safe, she hoped.

I tried to leave but had no idea how to read a map or anything and I wasn't going to call my mom & dad that was for sure, so I took her advice and sold my watch and rings to get some money for my trip. My husband knew that I really meant to leave and go back to Canada, he said ok we will go back just give me a day to buy a car and we will head back, I said ok if you mean it, I will wait for a day no longer or I am out of here, one way or another.

The one day came and went, and then the second day he drives up in this really nice car, a Dodge Charger, it was a very nice car but needed a little work, there was some rust and the lights kept going on and off, so I guess that meant a wiring problem, but it ran great. I asked where did you get this? He said from a car lot. Where did you get the money for it? I said. He replied; I didn't pay any thing for it, you did, it is in your name. Oh my word what is wrong with you, I don't have any money and I didn't even go there, you did. No, I didn't, as far as they know it was you. Well how can they say I was there? I wasn't there and you don't look like a girl or me? He said; I had a friend go with me and sign as you, that's how. I was horrified that I was going to get in trouble along with everything else that was going on too. You have to take it back and we will get out of here some other way, I can't he said, I set the place on fire so they can't trace the papers and who really bought the car. I turned the radio on. The news said, the car lot burned to the ground, the owner had a heart attack and was in critical condition in the hospital. I was devastated and scared to death, what am I going to do now, if he dies I know who caused it and also that he would make it sound like it was me, that is what he was like. I didn't know what else to do but get the hell out of there and hope to get back to Canada and deal with it there, so we set out to come back home.

We went to his mother's place and stayed there. She was so nice to me I had to confide in her what had happened and ask what should I do? Her reply was" that bastard he will never learn", I never raised my son to be like that, whatever possesses him do these things, it isn't the first time he has been in a mess.

The next day my husband and I went down town and looked around for a job. We were told by his mom, not to take the car so we didn't, but when we came back the car was gone, he was raging mad, where is the car she said you never mind it is gone and you will never find it. I will not have a car at a house that could cause all of us to go to jail because of you and what you did. He replied; what I did! Did Deb tell you that? She said no, a birdie told me, and by the way, that man that had a heart attack also died today. If they come looking for you, I will hand you over to them, but not Deb she didn't do any thing, you're just getting every one involved with your stupid scams and I will not stand for it any longer. You need to grow up, but that would be a miracle. We never heard anything about it again and went on with our lives, if you want to call it that.

I had received a job at Kentucky fried chicken. Thinking everything was going to be all right, it was a fulltime job, and I like cooking. The job didn't last too long because this one woman reached over top of me to grab a lid for the pressure cooker, her hands were covered in grease and when she grabbed it, it fell causing the pot I was holding, to splash into my eyes. They called a cab and sent me to the hospital, where they bandaged both eyes and said they didn't know if I would be able to see again they were burnt so badly. Six weeks down the road they took the patches off and I could see, that made me happy, but I have some sad news I didn't get my job back. They tried to say it was my fault. What else is new, everything is my fault.

He got a job at a retirement home as a cook and started taking pills from the residents. He came home one day all stoned yelling and screaming that I was no good and he was going to kill us meaning his mother and I, he came in the house and packed some of his clothes And began marching up and down in front of the house yelling and screaming out of his mind police came and took him to the hospital and released him 24 hours later. He said it was from someone putting something in his drink, we knew that was a lie because his boss called and had to fire him for stealing.

I found another odd job, sounding the slip at the grainy, for the ships to be able to get in and out. It was winter, mid December, and I didn't have winter clothes to wear, but that didn't matter to me, I wanted to work and have money for Christmas, the job was only for two weeks, it was important to me not to have to borrow any money for the gifts. I felt it wouldn't be from me if I did not pay for them my self.

The first day of work, I went out in the boat to sound the slip and got soaking wet, my hands were freezing and I didn't have gloves to wear, my pants were frozen with ice hanging off them, I didn't have a winter coat, it was a fall jacket I could hardly move from being so cold and wet. I made it through the first day and went home and my mother in-law was mad at me for doing this with improper clothes and said, "You're going to catch your death of foolishness girl". The next day I was sick with a cold but didn't tell any one and went to work. The same thing happened and even my boss commented on the way I was dressed, again I was froze and covered with ice but again I made it through the day only feeling like I was going to die with the cold and all. I went home and again my mother in-law came down on me like a ton of bricks and said you are not going back to that job, you are too sick. I was running a fever by this time it was 103 something. She called a cab and took me to the hospital and they kept me in for 2 weeks, they said I had double pneumonia. I was so upset because I didn't have money for gifts, but there was nothing I could do. I got out of the hospital and found another job at customs border crossing unloading raw cow hides from one trailer to another, boy that was the smelliest job I ever did and the heaviest. The hides were 75 lb to 100 lb each and had to pile them on fridge dollies to transport to the other trailer and very slippery too from the salt, maggots and slime from the rotting hides. The third day I was taking a load over to the other trailer when I lost my footing and went down with the load on top of me, that meant a weight of 5x100= 500 lb was on top of me I started to bleed internally, they took me to the hospital and had to operate to stop the bleeding and that is when my husband signed for me to have a complete hysterectomy because I had endometriosis really bad, they said that if they didn't do this then I wouldn't live more than two years, but what they didn't tell me was there was a pill out that I could have taken and been fine, anyway my husband signed for a complete hysterectomy and that was the end of me ever having children. I hated him and kids for a long long time. I felt my life was really over now, I didn't think my life could've gotten any worse than it was before the surgery, but it did and all I did is drink and take drugs to forget everything and it was working, in my brain, not reality, it was destroying my thoughts, beliefs and future.

Finding That He Was Married To Two Other Women

What a beautiful day, I said to my mother-in-law when I had got up that morning and sat down at the table for my cup of coffee. Then the day started to get dim from the news she was going to tell me. Deb she said, sit down I have wanted to talk to you now for a while but I couldn't get up the courage and now I feel you must know. My son has deceived you from the beginning, he is married and he isn't the age he told you either, and he was never in the army or war or any of that what you were told, I am sorry I never told you sooner. His first wife lives here in Canada and had 3 children and his second wife and 4 children, lives in Beaverdam, KY. I said I knew he has an ex-wife in KY, but didn't the one in Canada. Well she said he isn't divorced from the one here in Canada yet, wow that was a shock. She said you know the young lad that has the same name as my boy. That comes over every so often, that is his son from the first marriage. Then he lied to me, he said; just a friend that had the same name, he was our witness, and we were his at the double wedding. They both said they were not related, when they were asked from the minister and the marriage licence place this is making me go nuts, I can't believe I have been so dumb, my dad was right saying I was too dumb to be on my own. I sure didn't feel like living that was for sure, it always came back to that feeling of being better off dead so I wouldn't have to live like this, this is the worst thing, living. Nothing in my life was worth living. Every thing went wrong from being born, marriage, work, family (what's that). I couldn't understand the purpose of life, what was there to live for, I certainly wasn't happy, every one said; you have to be happy in life, well that wasn't happening by a long shot.

I asked a lawyer, what could I do to get out of the marriage? My husband was married to two other women and me. He had a divorce to the second wife, and I was the third. He said well you're not legally married then and you have to get an annulment not a divorce. I asked what name I go by. He said; either one for now, we have to go to court and get this done. The weeks went by, I didn't hear from the lawyer. I called him and he informed me the only way it could be done was that I had to prove what I was saying was true. Get the names and addresses of the other women; also prove he or they (the wives) hadn't applied for a divorce from him. Where in the world am I going to get this type of info, he said research. Wow, I didn't know the first thing on how to get this done. He told me that he could not do any more for me until I had that information.

I had no other option than to stay with the idiot, welfare wouldn't help me because I was married to him as far as they were concerned and was to stay with him till proven different, he was denying he was married to other women and also had a good job at the time.

The dilemma continued for a couple years then I said I had enough and took an overdose to end it for good this time. I almost made it. They took me in the emergency room and started all the Intervenes lines, in both arms & oxygen. They found out it was too late to pump my stomach. I tried to rip out the IV that is when they tied me to the stretcher, all they could do was hope that I didn't take enough, but again the angels around me stopped the attempt. The dr. had taken blood work and said I had enough to down a horse but I came through. Dam I didn't want to come back; I was fighting so hard not to live the Dr said that my adrenalin kicked in and saved my life. That was the only thing that he could think of. They transferred me to the psychiatric ward for help and I didn't give them much cooperation either, I was done I didn't want this life or have help. I felt everyone was against me and were out to harm me in some way, everyone was an enemy, I refused to eat and take any medication. I couldn't sleep and was getting violent with anyone that came close.

I thought if I pretended I was getting better that they wouldn't watch me so close and it worked, now I would do this right, all I needed was a sharp blade and follow the vein not cut across it and they wouldn't save me then ha! ha! I got it now, that scheme made me so happy. I was so good they gave me a two-hour pass, now is my chance to get the blade. I went out got it and came back all smiles, I guess that must have given it away, they searched me and I ended up losing my temper again, they found it and that was not a good thing. They put me in this little room with only underwear on. I was verbally and physically abusive to the staff and myself. All of a sudden, the door flew open and this needle came at me, I turned away but it hit me in my hip, I pulled it out and threw it at the door. I sat down and that was the last thing I remember that day.

The door came open again and I was scared that some thing was going to be thrown at me again but that didn't happen I was calmer and didn't want to fight with them any more. They took me back to my room where the nurse sat and talked with me, she was very nice and understanding , she said to me that I was more harm to myself than to any one else and that they just wanted to help me. Help me! I don't want help; if you people hadn't stuck your face in, I wouldn't be here. I wouldn't have to go through this again, why is she being nice, and what does she want? She is going to try to trick me some how, I just know it. I started to get agitated again because of this and they came in with some pills, I took them, but things just kept escalating, so then they brought in a needle and my temper flared again, they held me down and gave me the shot, which put me out for another day.

The next day, I was woken up, by a big man leaning on my chest, slapping my face yelling at me, wake up, wake up. My face was sore and I went nuts what the hell do you think your doing, get the hell off me you pig, I have been trying to wake you up, I am your psychiatrist, you took some drugs after we gave you medication didn't you? I said no you guys gave them to me last night, he replied we didn't give you enough to knock you out like that. He didn't believe me, so I just shut up and didn't say a word this is just like when I was at home with my dad, you don't argue, it doesn't get anywhere, it just gets you in more trouble and I didn't want that to happen.

As the days went by, I calmed down enough so they could talk to me without my temper going off. I wasn't eating or drinking, thinking they would put some thing in it. So the Dr. was always threatening me that they would put an IV in so I wouldn't get dehydrated, to me that was their idea to give me some thing else in the IV like valium or another type of drug, because I refused to take any medication. I was very angry, and confused. A person that thought the world was out to get me. I figured I was this dumb, ugly, girl that didn't deserve to be on this planet with all the normal people. Why are they making me stay here? Is it for experiments? Just to see what makes me tick or some other reason, I just didn't understand that my life was messed up from the beginning and wasn't from my doing, it was from what had happened to me in my younger years and was snowballing out of control.

This one nurse came in and talked to me every few hours, some times every ½ hr. I started to talk to her after about 2 weeks of her just saying any thing that was on her mind, like things that happened in her life and people around her. She was the one woman that started me thinking on the right track, the psychiatrist wasn't helping at all. The psychiatrist Dr said I had to get over it and quit taking so much drugs, drugs I said I haven't taken any thing since I came in here, yes you have he said, just admit it and we can help you. Well I hate to burst your bubble Doc but the only things I have taken is your pills that you and the nurses force me to take and I am not going to admit some thing I didn't do. That is the problem every one looks at me and automatically think I am on or taking drugs so why shouldn't I do it because I am being accused of it any way. All my life I was accused of some thing that wasn't true, I am sick of it. Your husband told us you were heavy into drugs that is why we are treating you in that manner, I started to laugh, see that is just what I was saying , did you take blood test to confirm it, he said; we took blood but it came back negative, laughing even harder I said and you still believe him. Why should I trust you? Or anyone else for that matter. He asks me, are you going to try and commit suicide if we let you go? I said I can't say I will never try but I wouldn't right now.

Why do you want to kill your self? Well life sucks and so does the people in it, is that good enough. Why do you think the people suck? I haven't been able to find one person that wasn't out to do harm to others, in some way or another. They say they're your friend and would like to help, just give me a call they would say, when you do call, they are either nasty to you or start calling you names. Some steal your stuff from you when they come to your house. You can't tell anyone anything personal, because they tell every one else and then people think you're a sick mental reject. I am not going to go all through my life looking over my shoulder wondering, if what I told some one is going to come out and bite my ass. The Doc said to me "I think you are exaggerating, people aren't that bad", I couldn't help it I started to laugh and said you are the nut job and I am never going to tell you any thing because I don't trust you, and I don't like you either. He said maybe I should refer you to some one else then, I said well what ever you want, that doesn't mean I will say any thing to them either. (That same psychiatrist years later shot himself and his wife) I was sent to another person to talk to and it was a woman but she could only say talk about it and we can work on it and my response was ok, so I told her about my father being abusive to the animals and she said I was to forget it and start living now not back then. I knew right then, she was not the one for me to tell any thing of my past.

I was in the hospital for a whole month and didn't feel any better. I did decide not to go back in there again, no matter how bad I got. It was no help at all, and they didn't believe what I had told them. The pills were worse than the problem, as far as I was concerned, I couldn't think properly, I kept wondering if I was dreaming every thing or was it true I couldn't tell and that made me more depressed than I was.

The last week I was in the hospital the nurse that I could talk to came to me and said that they were going to send me to the women's interval home, I ask why? She said you want to get away from your abusive husband don't you? Yes I do but what is this place your sending me, is it like jail or some thing, she busted out laughing and said no it is where women & children go to be safe from their abuser, oh I said and then we started to talk about what he was like, my husband or what ever he was, I was confused about who he was and what I was, am I really a bad person or is the world bad, either way I still didn't want to live in it, but I had made a promise to her that I wouldn't try killing my self until I called some one that I trusted. Well that would be a long time because I didn't trust any one at that time.

It was the day to move to the home for abused women. I was scared not knowing what was going to happen, because my husband said he was going to kill me if he couldn't have me for himself but he wasn't really my husband either according to my lawyer.

Staff at the center was nice, maybe too nice, I shouldn't do too much talking till I know that they're not going to send me back to the hospital. I wasn't there two days when this lady came up to me and said how do you feel today Deb, in a snappy tone, why! Who are you any way? She said my name is so & so and I just wanted to see how you were doing that's all. I said I was sorry for being so mean and she said; I can understand, you have been through a lot lately, apology is accepted, and she sat down beside me. She asks me what my husband was like and I told her the completely confusing story about him but not my past.

It didn't take long for them to find out first hand what his intentions were going to be, he called about 20 times the third day and demanded to talk to me and told them I was telling them a bunch of lies. He would come to the security door and ring the bell for 5 to 6 min then go to a phone booth and call and call. All this time they were telling me what he was doing, and I was getting scared. Thinking that they would kick my butt out, and say they didn't need that kind of trouble around, but that didn't happen they said you just leave this up to us, we will call the police if we have to, don't you worry he will not be able to get in or hurt you. The next day one of the staff took me to the courthouse to get a peace bond on him so I could at least go out for some fresh air and not be afraid of being, beaten up.

After getting the peace bond in place, I decided to go down town to meet a friend for coffee. My friend and I were having a good time talking and he walked in knowing that I was there. He came over and sat down, what you up to? I replied having a coffee. You're not supposed to be here or near me or my friends. he said with a grin and chuckled, you think a piece of paper is going to stop me, I said it will I am calling the cops, he replied; I will be gone before they get here, go right ahead and call them. He got up, smacked me on the head, and said you will regret this; you know that don't you and left. My friend called the police and they came down, interviewed us, and said there wasn't enough to charge him but they will go talk to him. I never went out for almost two weeks. Within the two weeks I never went out a private investigator came knocking at the door. He asked for me, and told the staff he needed my help with the case he was working on. I asked him what type of case, he replied; the little girl that was hit with a car July the fourth, Seven years ago you were a witness to. I said that was a long time ago, he said do you remember it. Yes! I remember what happened, but before I tell you, can you help me on something. He replied I will see, and I began to tell him my dilemma, my husband was married twice before and I need proof in order for me to get an annulment from the Supreme Court of Ontario. Do you think you can help me? I will help you. He responded and said, not a problem. Then I began to explain it was the little girl's fault, not the man that was driving, she ran right into the side of the car, he did not run over her, and then she went under his back wheel of the car. I remember the lady the little girl was with yelling come back, come back, the little girl yelled back saying I can make it and then she hit the front side of the car. I had nightmares for a long time after that happened. I felt it was my fault because I was running across the road in front of her, not waiting for an opening in the traffic, like I should have. After we finished with my statement he said he was going to get back to me on his findings with my husband's wives. We shook hands and he left. I really didn't think he would ever look for my husband's ex-wives and flushed it from my thoughts, thinking I would never get out of this marriage alive any way.

I knew he would continue his threats. He was told by the police many times not to call the woman's home, but he didn't listen. The police never did enforce the peace bond, I knew that I was doomed just like I was with my father, but this time I was determined not to go in hiding even if it cost my life, I didn't care any more if he did kill me, I was tired of every thing.

I was talking to the staff at the center about what had happened and they even called their lawyer, there was nothing at that point to do. Well they talked me in to getting an apartment for myself, and they would help get me started by giving me pots, pans, dishes, etc. and some food. It was moving day again and they assured me he didn't know where it was, because he would try and follow us when we went out.

The apartment was cute, hidden in the back of a house so I couldn't be seen from the street, there was a kitchen bathroom and a bedroom, just big enough for one person it was great, I was finally on my own and a little scared, but happy at the same time, a weird feeling one I hadn't felt before.

I was very carful not to be followed looking over my shoulder all the time. I felt like people where watching me all the time. I didn't like that, it wasn't right that I had to be the one always running. The police and courts should be able to do some thing, so I could at least have some safety in my own home, but they kept saying there was nothing they could do until he did some thing, like break in the house or beat me up. Well that is what he did the next week, I was having a snooze around 2 pm and the door flew open, with a big crash the window shattered, glass went flying and I jumped to my feet and he knocked me down, pounding me like a mad man, then smashing every thing he could find to smash, he lunged at me again and I put my feet up on his chest and pushed as hard as I could, he went flying and right in to a part of the wall that was sticking out, he was hurt, and I didn't stop I started to throw things at him, it was either him or me and I had a part of me saying get'em and he ran out. I was scared and shaken when the police came, my landlord called them, but again they did nothing, but I was told I had to move out, they had enough and they couldn't tell the cops who it was because they didn't see him they only heard the noise and didn't want to get involved.

I really don't think I was meant to be on this earth I was a mistake from the beginning. The women shelter helped me again to move back with them. They had me all settled in when the crap started all over again, him phoning, banging on the door, ringing the buzzer and them calling the police to have it stopped, but he would only stop for a couple days and start all over again.

I told them I have to go out and get a job and do some thing; this is driving me nuts sitting here day after day. I went out to look for work and made a big mistake and ask my ex if I could borrow his car for an interview I had to get to , he seemed happy to do that and handed me the keys, I left , had my interview and came back to give him the car, he was not in the best of moods at this point, he thought I would only be an hour and then I would stay with him and live happily ever after, but that wasn't my thoughts, he grabbed me and started to choke me and hit me in the face, I saw a cop across the road and screamed Help! Help! The cop yelled back it is a domestic dispute lady and started to walk away, I lost all fear and gained some strength, weaselling out of the hold, he had me in, I kick him hard in the you know what, as he was bending over from the pain, my boot came up and kicked his head. I saw the blood fling from his head and face, but I was so angry at this point, I kept kicking him and hitting. Then some thing told me to stop, I seen he was not moving, lying on the ground, I started to walk away and that same cop that was across the street came over and said are you going to call an ambulance, I turned and said 'sorry it is a domestic dispute' and walked away. When I arrived at work they looked at me and said you have to go to the hospital you're bleeding, I replied it's not mine it is my ex's and told them what had happened. The next thing you know, the intensive care unit was calling, asking me to come over. My husband was ranting & raving, thinking I could settle him down. I told them it was me that put him there and didn't want to talk or be around him, the nurse said he has a broken noise, rib, punctured lung and fractured jaw, all I could do was laugh and he couldn't even charge me because the cop was there.

He eventually was released from the hospital and started again only with a twist this time, he came to the door, rang the buzzer and said if you don't come down here now I am going to kill my self right here and you will never get over it. The staff said, don't go down there he is bluffing, he wouldn't do it, I said, yes he will I know him, he is nuts, believe me he is. Well the director went down to the door to talk to him, he was lying on the sidewalk, blood coming out of the side of his head, he must of hit the step when the drugs he had taken to kill himself kicked in. She called for an ambulance and police. The ambulance took him back to the hospital, where they had to pump his stomach. The police came over to talk to us about what had happened and then charged him with trying to commit suicide, I started to laugh and said; you can charge him for that but can't for beating the crap out of me and stalking me, they said; yes that's right. The court ordered 28 days in the psychiatric ward, but they kept him for 37 days, I enjoyed him not coming around and I also felt safe for the first time in my life.

Now I could get on with my life and be somewhat happy. I was getting ready to go out, get a job, then find a place to live. The Director came up to me and asked if I would be willing to live there and work the night shift because they had to cut back on the staff at night, the funding was not enough to pay some one to stay at night, I agreed and I had my own room and was on call all night. This worked out great until the funding from the government came in. The government wanted the staff to have a degree, which I didn't have, they did ask me if I wanted to stay on as a relief worker, if the regular staff needed a day off I could work and they would pay me a minimum hourly wage, I said that would help. I felt betrayed because I had worked four long years of my life and dedicated it to the women's home and now I can not be any help just because I don't have a degree. I knew everything that all the others knew and asked if I could take a test to acquire my degree their answer was no, I had to go to school, well that blew that because I didn't have a grade twelve. I was also working at the buses for the board of education, so it wasn't too bad, as far as work and income.

Going Back To School To Prove I Was Smart

I found a place to live and asked a friend if she would like to share the cost and be roommates, she agreed. We moved in together and had a great time. She was working and I found another job driving school bus, because both jobs were part time (when needed). I ended up being a charter bus driver for the board of education, driving the kids to school and going to different places for school trips. I remember this one trip, down to Windsor; it was a wrestling tournament for the high schools. I didn't feel that bad in the morning, but by noon I was really sick, all the other bus drivers had noticed, I had turned white and was not very talkative. They ask me how I was feeling, I said not well, but I could make it back. I did make it back, but I thought that my whole body was on fire I had a hard time to breathe. I started backing the bus up into its parking spot when one of the other drivers came along and said I will do it for you. They had called an ambulance and I was taken into the hospital and found out I had pneumonia.

It took me awhile to get over that and then came back to work.

I had decided that now that I had three jobs and a place to live that was safe, now I would go back to get my schooling at the adult learning center. That was a chore to juggle all of them because the school wanted me to be there more than I could be, can you believe they wanted me to quit working and go back full time, I said; how can I do that! I have to live, pay bills, food, and rent. They said if you want a full time job you're going to have to get your grade twelve, now what! Is this a joke I can't quit my jobs. I sat down and thought about it and the only thing that kept running through my head was, Dad said I was too dumb and so did my ex that I would never accomplish any thing in my life, is it true?, maybe I wasn't supposed to have a good job or have my schooling. My head started to pound, light & sound were driving me nuts, I was getting a migraine. I knew if I let it go too far I would pass out from the pain, it happened before. I went to the emergency department, they took an x-ray and saw the brain tumour and gave me an injection of some kind and told me to go to my family Dr the next day. That wasn't going to happen, me go to the Dr! I have to work. I know about the tumour and migraines, I didn't need a Dr to tell me what I already know. The Dr's keep telling me there is nothing they can do for the migraines other than pills, or an injection or operate and take the tumour out with a 50/50 chance of survival, mentally that is. That isn't what I had in mind, now that I have a little better life. I need to talk to some one that could understand my predicament and give me a suggestion or two.

I went to a psychologist to see if that would work, hmm she seemed very nice and understanding. I told her about wanting to go to school, needed to work and my ex-husband. She did help and said that I really needed to continue with school, I ask her? How can I go to school and survive with no work, her reply was, the unemployment would help with that if I had enough weeks to qualify for assistance. I was happy now I could go get my schooling and still have a place to live and food, I could not ask for any better than that. The unemployment made an appointment for me to come in and then they did some tests, to see what I would be good at, I didn't think I was good at anything and told them they didn't need to do the test, and I just needed to get my grade 12. The man said, no we need to do this, you come back in the morning tomorrow and we will get this done and then we will know what level you're at and what your qualities are. This is over my head, I don't know what qualities I have, or what they are and this made me very scared. The next morning I was there for my test, scared half to death and shaking out of my boots, the man came over and said you're shaking what's wrong? you don't need to be scared, it is just to see what level your at and what you like to do, oh I said, he chuckled and said every one gets nervous, but once they get started every thing works out fine, you will see. He handed me the papers and a pencil, he said you have 4 hrs to complete the test, but we will be taking breaks ok, I said that's ok. There was a whole bunch of answers to one question, am I to guess at this? Is there a right and wrong to these, what am I going to do, I don't get this, how can there not be a right and wrong? This is stupid and I might as well leave right now before they find out how dumb I really am, and put me in a hospital for the mentally ill just as my Dad said would happen. Just as I was walking out the guy came in and said, ok now every thing is ready for you to start, well I couldn't leave now, I guess I will have to do what I can and hope for the best.

I finished the tests with flying colors, wow that was easy. The tester came in with the results; it sure wasn't what I was expecting. There was no right or wrong. He told me that I was a very smart and talented person. My first response was to tell him he needed to check to see if he had the right test and not some one else's. I didn't say any thing, if he wanted to tell me that, I would go along with it, this might be to my advantage to let him think I was smart, even though I didn't think I was. He told me I could be a nurse, cook, labourer, police woman or in the military, wow that was a shock the test had to be wrong, I could never be any of them, maybe a cook but not the rest. I agreed to go back to school to get my grade 12, then after that I would decide whether I wanted to go in to other courses to further my career, if I even had one.

I started back to school at the community college. It was hard at first to concentrate, but I got used to it after a week. I loved math, it seemed so easy, why was it so hard and I didn't understand it when I was in school before, hmm. My first test, wow I was scared I thought I would look like a fool when it came back, it would be all wrong and I will fail. I was wrong it came back with a comment at the top with a smiley face that said very very good 98%. I was so proud and happy, I never did that before and I did it all by myself. The teacher came to me after class and said Debbie if you need any help just come to me and I will help you, I replied thank you I will. The next 6 months were the same, I never went under 80% on any of my tests. School was too easy, what is wrong? Are they just doing this to make me feel good or maybe it is for the money, there is some thing not right, I couldn't be this smart. I had to see if they would pass me if I wrote the wrong things down, no my tests came back fail right across the page, then the teacher came to me and asked, what is wrong Deb you where doing so good? What's the problem? I said; I just wanted to see if it was true, was I doing well! On the other hand, were you doing it to make me feel good? She replied; why would you think that I was doing it just to make you feel good? I wouldn't do that because you would never learn. You did it all on your own, I did not go easy on you or any one else. I said; I have never passed with these kinds of marks, I couldn't understand how it could happen. The teacher sat down beside me and said in a soft voice, I think that you need to talk to a counsellor about this, you will feel better and come to an understanding why you feel this way, I will set up an appointment for you if you would like. I said; sure, that will be great thanks. I knew that I needed that help; I was getting more depressed as the days went by. When I talked to the counsellor, the topic was about school and being afraid of people, not of my past, I didn't think it had any thing to do with what was happening to me in school, so I didn't mention it.

Lunch times at the college, I usually sat by myself, scared to talk to any one or even look sideways, I would have panic attacks when some one would say hello how are you today or nice day out isn't it. My fear was starting to take over my life; I didn't feel safe, just like when I was at home with my father or living with my ex-husband. I felt like some one was going to do me harm in some way, either with words or physically.

I had a friend that sat with me occasionally, but he usually had to work on the college newspaper at lunch. This one day he came running through the cafeteria as if some thing was on fire, and said Deb you have to enter this contest, I can't do that I said. Yes you can he said, all it asks is for a poem and they're going to pick from the whole college and make a book out of the winners. I was so upset with him, he didn't leave it alone, so I grabbed a napkin and started to write, this is what I wrote:

Be Yourself

I am who I am.
I am what I am.
No one is me, and I am no one else.
For everyone is what they make themselves.
No one person can change us.
For we have to change ourselves.

Then I handed the napkin to my friend and said there! Are you happy now? It won't win so don't get all bent out of shape when they tell you. He took off like a rabbit saying yes it will you'll see, ya right I said, as I picked up my books and went to class. I couldn't seem to concentrate and I decided to go home, but that wasn't going to fix my problem, what I needed, was to see another type of counsellor, maybe that would help, it wouldn't hurt. I talked to the counsellor I was going to and asked her opinion on what to do or could she help me. In her opinion, I should see some one else, she didn't think she was helping me and I agreed.

Looking for some one to help me in a problem that I didn't understand is hard and near impossible to find, but I did. I would never go to a male counsellor or doctor if I could get away with it. The new counsellor seemed very understanding and I had good talks with her until one day she asks the big question, have you been sexually abused? WOW, my heart started to race and I said why do you ask that stupid question NO I yelled, she said ok then you have, I replied; what makes you think that? I haven't been, she said; by your response, you yelled it out, well you scared me with that question, how else was I suppose to answer you, it's not like I am asked that every day you know. She began to chuckle, that is how I know, most people will say; no that didn't happen, but you responded irrationally to the question. We talked for several weeks about the abuse. Why does it take so long to get it out of my brain? Why can't I just have shock treatments to forget, a lobotomy. Then she said an outrageous statement, "you liked it when your dad was rubbing his penis up against you didn't you". I walked out and never looked back. She was nuts to think that I would like being beaten and sexually abused, she had no right to even suggest some thing like that, I was only a kid when it happened.

I don't know what to think of counsellors' now, none of them seem to help, I guess I am just going to do what I can, on my own.

I went back to school and my friend came up to me and said, I told you! You would win, and have it published in the college book, and I said; really, it is! He responded yes it did. Well that made my day; maybe I could just fake the rest of my way through life, worth a try, nothing else seems to work. I couldn't commit suicide right on my own and didn't have what ever I need to forget the past or go on with my future, I felt like a failure at every thing I did. Well there was one thing that I accomplished and didn't even try and that is my poem, maybe I should read it and see what it said because I can't remember what I wrote, I wrote some thing just to get my friend off my back and didn't really know what I said in it. When I received the book, I read my poem and that is what started me on the road to be a better person so I was thinking anyway.

My X-hubby, What Ever He Is Came Back Into My Life

This isn't good when you're unannounced, so called husband is standing in the doorway of your classroom; I jumped up and went over and said what are you doing here? He replied; you're still my wife we are not divorced so you still have to do what I say, no, I don't have to do what you say, you're not any thing to me, you're just an idiot. He hit me and I went flying against the wall. They called the police and they took him in another room and me in a different room, he won again, he said I fell against the wall that he didn't hit me; the red mark on my face was from the wall scraping my face, so they told him to leave and not come back on the property. I knew that I was in for more trouble that I couldn't handle on my own, but I wasn't going to go in to hiding the rest of my life either. I gave up; I felt I would never be able to be alone with out some one being over me, my life anyway. My x-husband came over to my house where my friend and her boyfriend lived so we could try and talk, but that didn't work either, he had phoned the college and told them I wouldn't be back. Then he wouldn't let me go to school the next day, by saying the school phoned and they kicked me out for being too much of a problem, that they didn't need the other students that wanted to learn, disrupted, I believed him. Then that same week my friend and I went out, letting the guys sleep so we could have a coffee and do girl talk. It was nice for a change; we talked about her and her boyfriend, how to get my ex-hubby out of my life.

We were walking back home when we heard the police sirens passing us, we began to laugh, saying too bad it couldn't be my ex-hubby keeling over, he would be out of our lives for good then. We arrived home with the police at the door and my friend's boy friend almost dead by my ex-hubby strangling him. I went in a rage, yelling, where is that idiot, I will kill him my self; I am done with his bull crap. I can't deal with this any more, I am going out of my mind. The police said calm down it isn't as bad as it looks, I looked at him and said, now that is a typical response coming from a man that hasn't a clue what this idiot had done for many years. I began to give them a short version of what he done in the past. The police went and found him and asked why he tried to strangle my friend's boyfriend, he said because he turned all the hydro off and I was cooking my breakfast that's why, well that wasn't the truth the fuse panel was in our bed room not theirs, and my friend's boyfriend, he was sound a sleep. My ex promised not to beat him up if he could stay for just a few more days, we all agree, thinking if we held off we would get him out with out a bigger fight.

I started to take the harder drugs, like cartoon acid, purple microdot, and H. I only tried that H once. My theory is if I can't make them believe me, I might as well do it. I was drinking 6-40 oz a week and taking the drugs too, I was working in a gas station at the time I was drinking, and no one even knew I was drunk 98% of the time or stoned out of my head. I was feeling no pain, after a month living in another world and planet, I knew it wasn't what I wanted to do, I hated my self even more, I had to change something, and get back to reality, what I thought was reality. My friend found the booze hidden under the sink in the kitchen and asked if I knew who's it was, I told her it was her boyfriends and felt bad for blaming him, but I didn't want her to know it was me either, that caused a big fight between them and they split up.

Finally, my ex-hubby moved out and went back to Kentucky, wow I was happy he has gone, hopefully for good.

I decided to stop all the drugs and booze and my body just wouldn't let me, but I was determined at this point to stop, so I went to a counsellor for drugs and alcohol. I have to be normal it is what I want. The counsellor said to me, you have to be honest with your self, and me if you want this to work, are you willing to tell the truth. I said yes I am but I can't stop, she said, yes with the right help you can, but the only thing I ask of you is, do not come here drunk or high, if you do I will ask you to leave. Then she asked me if I had taken any thing today, I had to be truthful I said yes and then she asked me what it was, she knew it wasn't booze, I said some pills the Dr. gave me, valium. She said; why are you on that? Well the Dr., he thinks I need them. She just smiled, and asks me to come back in two days, with out being high. I said; but I am on this medication, yes, you can take it, but not more than what is says on the bottle to take, as you are now. I said; but I wasn't feeling anything, so I took more so I would know it was working, she chuckled and said you don't have to feel it for them to be working. I said no one told me that, I am telling you now she said and I left.

This counsellor was different from the others, she smiled, laughed, accepted coffee, took me out to lunch, wow what is wrong with this one? I couldn't believe that I felt I could trust this one and started to question why. She was teaching me in a way I could understand. She told me I was a master manipulator and we were going to work on that as well. She felt it wasn't my intention to use it, she believed I didn't even understand what it meant, well she was right there, I didn't have a clue what she was talking about. It didn't take me long to learn, my appointments were the same every week, time, place. Some times, I would go early just to see if I could get longer time, but that didn't work. I started to question why did I like her so much, was I a lesbian, and was I in love with her? She reassured me that I wasn't and nether was she. I had feelings I never knew I had, she even took me out to a restaurant to eat and that alone scared the crap out of me, I never went out to restaurants if I could help it , too many people were there to watch me and I had a problem with that.

I was always dressed in black and kept to the closest door in case some thing ever came up that I needed to get out. My counsellor taught me there was nothing to fear, that with other people in restaurants, all they wanted to do was eat too and some would look around just to see if they knew any one there that was all. No one was out to get me, but I came back with the answer yes there is, my father knows every one and my ex-hubby too. The next appointment she asks me about my father and my ex-hubby and I finally told some one that believed me, wow this counsellor was good. She said this one appointment,"would you be willing to go to rehab for your drinking and drug use?" I immediately said yes, thinking that I could get away from my so called ex husband as well as get help that I desperately needed, yes I would like that, so she made the arrangements and I went there for a month. I learned a lot while I was in treatment. They gave me this pill to take every day call Antabuse, and told me if I had even a drop of alcohol it would make me deathly ill, I believed them. I was so tempted to go out drinking and doing the things I so desperately wanted to quit doing, the Antabuse necklace I was wearing stopped me, and I was glad. This gave me more hope for my future. About a month after getting out of rehab, I came down with a very bad cold and cough, and went to my Dr. to see what I could take for it, because I knew I couldn't buy cough medicine at the drug store, it had alcohol in it. The Dr. gave me a prescription and said take two tsp. every four hours; I asked him if it was ok with the Antabuse and he reassured me, it was ok. Well I went home and took my cough meds and not even 5 minutes later I was burning up, throwing up and getting red blotches as well, my friend called an ambulance and off I went to the hospital, they said you have been a bad girl you were drinking weren't you? I couldn't say any thing other than shake my head NO, but they didn't believe me. My friend came in and told them, "she didn't drink any thing I was there, all she took was the prescription cough medicine the Dr. gave her not even an hour ago". Then I saw them go nuts on me, putting Intravenous in , one in each arm and a oxygen mask and kept saying you're going to be ok, do you understand us, we are sorry we didn't know it was a prescription your friend just told us, you will be feeling better in a few minutes. They had the intravenous on full drip, it was cold going in my arms and painful too. I started feeling better, able to talk. They told me what they usually do, to patients when they have been drinking, when they shouldn't have been. They monitor the patient letting them go through some of the effects. Therefore, they would be deterred from drinking while on Antabuse again. That is why they didn't do any thing with me when I came in, until they found out I was telling the truth. The Dr in the emergence department said, what was your Dr thinking, all cough medication have alcohol in them unless you specify on the prescription NO ALCOHOL, I am going to call him and give him a talking to, you didn't need to go through this. After all was said, they released me and I went home to get some badly needed rest, still feeling like crap.

My appointment with my alcohol & drug counsellor was the next day. I decided that I wanted a picture of her, to have, because she was so nice and understanding. I wanted it to be a surprise, one that was natural not posed. I hid behind some bushes that was out in front of the building, she was to meet me at the coffee shop down the street, and when she came out the door I jumped up and took the picture, she screamed and scared me and I screamed, not realizing what happened we both started laughing. She said I thought you where shooting me, well that made me laugh even harder (hysterically), trying to say no I just wanted a picture. After I had settled down, she said, why did you want a picture of me. I replied I like you and wanted it to keep; she smiled and said you scared me, why didn't you just ask me? I would have let you take one.

She was a very good counsellor, she helped me with my drinking and listened to my problems, but she never told me what to do, always made me answer my own question, that also made me more confident in myself. She also taught me, not to believe every thing that was told to me, to trust my own thoughts not every one else's. She taught me not to manipulate people, even though I didn't know I was doing that, or what it was, she pointed it out, every time I did it to her, or told her what I said and did to some one else. I didn't want to say good bye, there was nothing more to say or talk about, the time had come when I had to end our time together. I had a hard time at first, I would walk by, wanting to just say hi and leave, but never did, I know I had to let go and carry on with my new way of dealing with life. I saw her every so often around town and said hi, and she would ask me how I was doing, I would always tell her I am doing great, even if I wasn't, I didn't want her to know I had failed again. I do a lot of failing in my life, can't find a full time job, never able to have a home, one to call home. I always seem to go into these bouts of depressions, that made me feel out of control or not able to do any thing, like I was lazy, but I am not a lazy person. When I would get angry, I felt I was going to lose it and hurt that person and maybe never come out of the anger, maybe even die if I couldn't control my feeling. I think that I am deceiving every one, when I tell them I am a good person and that I am smart, thinking to my self, why is that, I just feel I shouldn't be alive, I don't fit in this world with people, I am not like them and they're not like me, they are better, smarter, prettier, happier. The world would be better off with out some one like me. The thoughts are coming more and more the older I get. Why do I have to live like this? Well I decided to try, and start over and see if I was at fault for my failure as a human, not that I am an alien.

I was walking around in the park when my x-hubby came up to me, and asks if we could go for coffee and I agreed. We talk for a while then he asked if we could movie in together, only as room mates nothing else, well I said we never got along before why do you think we can now? He said; you do your thing and I will do mine; we just split the cost of every thing. We have done that before, I said and you stole the money and never paid, rent, groceries, and then bought all your buddies drinks at the bar with my money, we got booted out of the apartment and put in the credit bureau, you beat the shit out of me, now do you think I should forget that ever happened?. He replied; I have changed now, I'm not the same person you knew before. I really don't expect to see a change in you, after all these years, you never tried to change when we were together. I will try and give it six months and if it doesn't work then you're out. I will put the apartment in my name and you will be staying there as a guest. Do you agree to these terms? Because if you don't we're not moving together at all, ever.

We move in together and things seem to be all right for a while then he started his crap and again, stealing money, not paying his part of the rent and bills, doing everything he wanted to do. I became sick with a cold or flu and running a fever, I asked him to help me go to the doctor, he said no; I will go get your medicine you stay here, you're too sick to go out. I believe him again, he went to my doctor and got some antibiotics for my flu, but what he didn't tell me that it was the wrong antibiotic the one I am allergic to, I kept getting sicker, my throat and tongue started swelling I struggled to make it up to look at the pill bottle while he was gone out, and it said penicillin, I am allergic to it. That is why I am so sick and he knew that I was allergic to it; I figure he was trying to kill me and make it look like an accident. I phoned the doctor, and the doctor immediately sent a new prescription and told me to get rid of him that he would eventually kill me, because he knew from my past what he was like. I said; why would you give him those pills when you knew, it was in my file, that I had an allergy to that drug. He responded saying; your hubby told me that you had taken them before and you where not allergic, well I said you need to believe your patient not the rest of the world.

When my ex came back, I kicked his butt out and moved again, even though I was sick. My friend let me stay there, while I was getting better. My friend asks if I wanted to split on every thing and live with her, I said sure. Several months went by, when I decided to go to Toronto to school for trucking, and that would get me out of part time work where I was. I headed off for Toronto to go to trucking school, had nowhere to live so I stayed in a hostel, that was interesting, there were many people staying there because they had nowhere to live. I had never seen this before so I was frightened and nervous. I hope I don't make a mistake like they did and live on the streets I know what that's like. I went to the school for my A license but when I got there they said that I couldn't take it I had to go for the D license which I already held it didn't make any sense to me but who am I to dispute the school. I finished my schooling, my diploma for straight truck driver and moved back to my home but I could not get the job because I was a woman and according to them too short. So all the time I spent getting my license to drive truck didn't do any good until years later.

When I went back home I tried looking for an apartment and was not accepted unless I had someone to sign with me, there was no one else I could have asked. I had to break down and ask my so called husband if he would move into an apartment for short time, until I could get on my feet again, of course he agreed. This is when I finally found out he really was married to two other women. I went to the mail box and a letter was there for him from his ex wife. It was her divorce papers, I was so excited, I took them down to my lawyer's and had it photocopied, I finally have the proof and I could get my annulment. I brought the papers back home and gave them to my ex-husband

and he asked why the letter was opened my reply was I caught you, you bastard. I told you I would get you.

Did you believe that you would never be caught for this and we would always stay married? He never responded. When we went to my lawyer's, he told the lawyer that yes he was married to two other women one from Canada and one from USA and then me. He also told my lawyer that he'd rather kill me than let me go, he told him he would also kill himself. My lawyer said; there must be something wrong with that man, he just admitted to everything, beating you up, trying to poison you and admitted he is going to try to kill you. We're going to put a reconnaissance order on him for your safety. I replied; that won't help I've had them before and it never helped, police or anyone except for the women's shelter. When we went to court and he said in the court room, if I can't have her, no one else will either. He also said; you cannot get an annulment or a divorce if the person is insane and I am insane he said. Oh my god I am doomed, He was trying to claim he was insane. My heart dropped as they were doing the investigation. Once the investigation was over we went back to court and he was found not insane, that was great news. The judge ordered an annulment with no charges for bigamy, the judge said, I also can be charged for knowingly marrying him when he was married, the judge did not believe me that I knew nothing about him being married to other women. He was ordered to pay all court costs including my costs, which he never did pay, but I was so happy I was finally free from a marriage of captivity, abuse, verbal and sexual. To me I was also freed from society for making me stay with someone I was not legally married to. When I got home I had all his stuff packed ready to leave when he asked me; can you give me a month to be able to get an apartment of my own?. You have done that for me so I guess I am obligated to do it for you as long as you're out in a month. I don't want to ever talk to you again or see you. You have caused me to lose too much of my life and it's about time I got on with my life.

The month went by and he did move into his own place but that did not stop him from harassing me, calling me, and telling people, male friends that is that I was still his wife, just to scare them off so I would not get involved with anybody and maybe come back to him, but that's not going to happen as far as I'm concerned.

How I Eventually Got Rid Of My Ex-husband

A friend of mine and her boyfriend were having a baby. She was age twenty four and he was sixteen and asked me if I would adopt the child, I said no but I would help you raise the child. A child should be with their parents, there's nothing wrong with you so you should be looking after your own children she agreed.

She had a baby boy. While she was in the hospital she could not come up with a name, so she said to me, give me a name that you would name this child if he was yours, so I gave her a name I would name my own. The next day I came up the child's name that I wanted, I always felt he was like my own I took him out I played with him I did everything I could to make his life happy. Then one day she came over and told me she was having another child. I can't tell you what my feelings were. I am a believer, if there is no supporting partner there should not be any children, that is how I have lived, I have no children because I have no supportive partner, that I can count on and that the child would be OK. I never felt that I had security, confidence, and money enough to have a child. I also never felt I had brains enough to look after a child, I barely got by on my own and I didn't want a live on welfare. I decided I was going to join the military, the regular army, but that didn't work out they said I was too short and I didn't have enough education. So I went to the police to see if I could join there and the same thing happened, not enough education and two short, so my final trial was to go in the reserves and believe it or not, I was accepted. I went through the medical and all the other things. I started out in basic training. I loved it, it was exciting, and I was learning things I had never learned before. I learned in order to shoot someone you had to have no regrets, and be able to hold your feelings back. I came to believe that I could not shoot someone intentionally unless I was being attacked and made angry. I started to feel sensitive to different things that I was doing there, I knew I could not kill my father and why I couldn't kill him, I had feelings I never knew I had. I was not a murderer, but maybe I could in self defense. I graduated from basic training and was posted in a border town, where I was to go to meetings on Thursdays and sometimes on weekends. This is what I wanted. My next rank I was going for was corporal. I wanted to stay in this and have it as a career, but that was short lived. There again Life shot my dream down. I became sick with pneumonia and couldn't make it to two of the meetings. My Sergeant requested me to come and he wanted to talk to me, he gave me the option of a dishonorable discharge or a medical discharge, I'm not a stupid person so I took the medical discharge. I was so disappointed I had a note from my doctor stating why I hadn't been there and that I had not gone to school either because of being sick, but that didn't help with the Sergeant. Later on that year that same Sergeant was dishonorably discharged for urinating on the government steps while intoxicated. I felt betrayed, that I couldn't serve my country, and being discharged for medical reasons. I felt I was not given the opportunity to explain, and possibly rectify the problem if there was one. They never gave me any other reason other than I did not come to the meeting when I was supposed to even though I was sick.

She had a little girl by the same father of the boy. She was so cute but I could not get close to her as I have gotten to the boy because I felt I would have to look after and support the little one, like I had the boy. The child services were always involved, and I didn't feel that another child wouldn't be right at this point. A couple years down the road she was pregnant again with a little boy by a different father. Now she had three children two boys and a girl. The girl was the middle child.

My friend got involved with another man and child services got more involved and tried to take the boy and that is when I stepped in, my friend and I went to my lawyer and had a contract written up, stating I had full custody of her eldest boy until further notice, that I was leaving the country with him and when she wanted him back I had 48 hours to have him back in her home. I had been in his life from birth till he was six years old, we did everything together, I took him to work when he was newborn, we went to the park I put him in day care to be able to play with the other children his own age, I knew what it was like to play by myself with no other children and did not want him to go through the same thing. I could not see him taken away either. We left for Kentucky that night. I kept him safe from the clutches of child services, I couldn't handle them taking him away and for me never to see him again, because I was also in the system and never seen my parents ever again. My ex also came with me because that is where he wanted to live now that we're as separate individuals. I enrolled the boy into school and into an after-hours program where he thrived. Six months went by and the call came I want my son home she said. So off we went back to her home, after a year children's services stepped in and took the children away with visitations. The children's services used me as a pawn, telling her, you will have to get your friend Debbie to drive you if you want to visit your children because we don't have the resources to get you there. That put me in the middle because if I was working I would have to take off work in order to drive her for her visit and if I didn't the children would think I didn't love them so I had to do it. The visits sometimes were as far away as three hours' drive and she couldn't afford the gas she had two other children to look after.

I had enough of the Emotional roller coaster and decided to move to Toronto to work and live. Several months went by and the children were placed back home with their mother. This made me very happy as I said before, children should be with their mother and father. Then the most dreading phone call came, Debbie your ex husband's here and said he will kill us if you don't come, I was so upset, I never even thought of calling the police and said to him what are you doing I cannot make it there in an hour I live farther away than you think, he said; I don't care I will give you six hours to come or they're dead. I hung up the phone and went to a car rental, jumped in and headed out to save them; I could not have handled it if anything happened to those children or my friend, whom I had called my sister for many years. My ex husband, he must have gone off his rocker. It took me four and a half hours to drive there and he said; I wouldn't really have killed them I was saying that to get you to come back, I love you will you remarry me,

I said; not on your life you need to get out of my life, I hate you. I stayed in the town for several months renting because I had been laid off from my job In Toronto and figured I might as well get a job here, because I did not think I would be called back to work and I was right. The plant closed up and was sold not to reopen again.

There was a young girl that lived beside my friend she was only fourteen or fifteen at the time, we became friends she is a nice girl and is a friend to this day. I went to her mother and asked her if she could come with me, to take my ex husband to Kentucky, her mother agreed. She never asked any questions she never even knew who I was, but still allowed her daughter to come with me, I just shook my head in amazement that she would allow this. I rented a car and my little friend and I drove my ex husband down to Kentucky where he wanted to go, he said he would get out of my life forever if I'd just drove him, I thought it was a small price to pay to have him out of my life forever. My little friend and I had a lot of fun joking around and laughing all the way, my ex-husband didn't think any of it was funny, he didn't want me to bring her at all, but I knew if I brought her that I would be bringing her back home without him. We got into Kentucky around ten in the evening we booked into a motel to our amazement we were so overtired we giggled most of the night over anything. The next morning we went out and had breakfast and drove my ex around to find a place just to make sure he was going to stay. He was turning down everything he seen when I realized this I said the next place you get you take it because we're leaving whether or not you have an apartment. He did, it wasn't a bad place either pretty nice for the money. We said our goodbyes and hoped he had a good life, I said please keep your promise and stay away I need to get on with my life and you with yours.

Now we were on our way home my little friend and I. We arrived in Ohio to our amazement it was a blizzard, they had closed the roads down and said we had to stay at this motel, we had no money we had spent it all in Kentucky so we stayed in our car for a few hours. It seemed to get worse and I said we have to go no matter what we will just take our time. Jumping snowdrifts and laughing we headed out back to Canada. We came upon the border at Michigan and Sarnia they waved us through, so we wouldn't get stuck in the snow, not even stopping. If I hadn't known that we would not have to stop I would've got some stuff to bring back, but we did not know this was going to happen, and we made it back safe and sound. Everything was closed down, even the transit system was closed, we were so tired we had stayed up all that night driving through the snow we stopped off at Harvey's for breakfast I was so tired I threw the keys to the car in the garbage not thinking, my little friend and I were laughing so hard digging through the garbage looking for the keys. She has never let that down she teases me all the time about it. I drove back to my place and we crashed she fell asleep on the couch and I in my bed. The next day I decided I was going to do my income tax so I went to the taxation place with all my papers. They said, hi! How are you today? I said not bad. Then they inform me I could not do my income tax, my response was, why not? They told me my husband was in last week and did the income tax. What! I'm not married. Can you prove that? Yes. They said while you're going to have to bring us some proof. So I went home and got the annulment papers and brought the in. They looked at them and said well he claimed your kids I said what kids I have no children again they said can you prove that I said yes. I went to my doctor and got a statement stating I had a hysterectomy and never had any children. They said they were sorry that he had claimed our four children and me and the rent on the apartment, all I could say was you guys are idiots for not looking into it, you have been my taxation place for many years and you can't even remember that I was never with him I always claimed single with no children. He never claimed me before so why should you think that he can claim me now? Yes he has children with other women but not with me, not only that, he has never claimed his kids before, if you look at the records you would know that. She said well maybe he is claiming them, I replied not a chance they're too old, and they live on their own and have their own children now. Now what do I do? The tax lady said well, I have to talk to my supervisor to see what can be done, I said OK. They called me the next day and asked me to come in that they would do my taxes. When I went in they said that they had filed thirteen government charges against him and wanted to know where he was, I told them where he was, I'm not going to keep it a secret. The charges were working while drawing welfare and unemployment also claiming false claims on his taxes stating he was married with four children to me and the taxes that comes back on the rent. I asked them, how they are going to get their money back because they gave him cash back, and would I get my income tax cash back or do I have to wait. She told me they will get it back through the courts. Not to worry they will catch him someday, because they could not have him brought back from the United States, but when he crossed the border at any time they can nail him. I knew this was my chance, the minute he would cross the border to see me or come over I would turn him in. I'm finally freed of this idiot. The charges were finally out and waiting for him just across the border.

A couple years went by and his sister my ex sister in law gave me a call, she asked how I was doing and wanted to know if we could move in together and save some money, we always got along I said sure I don't mind, we arranged to move in together. We agreed that I would go to work and she was on disability so she would stay home and look after the house, do dishes, make supper. We had a lot of fun. We would go out to the movies or go on vacations together. She asked me if I would feel awkward going to Kentucky for a vacation I replied no I don't mind. So off we went to Kentucky I took her on the riverboat she loved it. And the thing we both dreaded was running into her brother my ex. We came up with a scheme and said I was remarried to a police officer and not to come near me or come back to Canada if he knew what was good for him. That must've scared him because he left us alone for the rest of our trip. I ask her why she did not like her brother very much and she disclosed to me that he had molested and raped her when she was a child, now things started to be clearer to me, why he chose me to be his wife; it was because I was so young, not because he really loves me. How can I be so stupid and miss all the signs. This is when other people had told me he did something to their child, things started to fall into place and I understood what had happened, it had taken me a long time to realize this. After she disclosed all this to me I started to feel responsible for everything that had happened to other children because of me. I started feeling my life Spiraling rolling downhill again and this time I could not control it. Everything that had happened I could have stopped but I didn't. I didn't know why, I didn't listen or understand or maybe I didn't want to understand at that time. I really didn't want to live knowing another child was molested because of me. I finally decided that there was nothing I could do at that time and I needed to get on with my life and maybe forget the past. We came back home from our vacation and I decided I was going to go back to school but I needed help to do this. I got a hold of the vocational rehab to see if maybe they could help me and they said yes. I went through the Craig Reading Institute and learned how to read again and write from grades one to grade nine because I am dyslexic. I also have a problem when there are Noises in the room I cannot hear what others are saying. I get very frustrated and fall to pieces. I found this out when they did all these tests, to find out how come I couldn't learn like other people. It's taken me many years to get this far and I have so far yet to go. I was going to the school to do all my learning all over again, I learned I'm not the person I was or thought I was. I am compassionate, loving, friendly and a caring person.

The Changes In My Life That Seemed Like The World Was Coming To An End

My little friend was finally grown up and moved across the road from me with her boyfriend. Every day she would come over to see how I was doing and maybe go have ice cream after I got off work. I was working for the board of education at the time as a bus driver and charter driver as well as relief worker at the women's shelter.

I decided I was going to go visit my mother that was in the hospital with three types of cancer and not expected to live, she didn't know anyone and it was Labor Day weekend just before school started so I knew I could go to visit her in the hospital and be back at work for the Monday morning. I didn't want to go by myself, so I took two little friends and thought I would take them to the CN Tower on the way back. We got to the hospital to see mom and she didn't open her eyes so the nurse came into the room and tapped her on the cheeks, her eyes popped open and scared the life of me, they were big round, sad eyes. That is when I decided to say goodbye to my mom because I knew she was not going to live long. I kissed her on the forehead and told her she will be going to a better place and that I love her. It was so hard for me to leave knowing I would never see her again only in a casket. I decided since I had the two boys with me my father would not do anything, so I went out and said I had seen mom and I was on my way home. I was wrong. He told the boys to go out side and play, while he and I talked. He said to me, I want to show you something of your mom's upstairs, I should've caught on but I didn't, we got upstairs and he grabbed a hold of me and threw me on the bed and said; one more time for old time sake. I was shaking, scared, I was bigger now, I thought I would be able to handle it, he started to put his hands in my pants and thank god the boys came in the house and hollered at me, he jumped up and said make them go outside. I replied no I'm leaving now with the boys, and I never want to see you again. I left the house with the boys and headed for Toronto to the CN tower. I didn't want the boys to see how upset I was, so I pretended everything was fine when deep down inside my guts were burning and my head was just busting, I was angry, upset at what had happened. We arrived at the CN tower and when up in the elevators, the boys were so excited they could see all around, they had never been so high. We went into the gift shop and I bought them each a souvenir and we headed home. I brought the boys home and they were so excited they told their moms how high they were up in the sky and they called my mom grandma and that she was so sick, I didn't tell the boys that she was going to die; I thought they were too young. I was still disturbed at what my father had done and I headed to my home after dropping the boys off. I had a phone message when I got in the door saying it was my aunt and then the phone rang again, this time it was my aunt calling to say her sister my mother had passed away. I didn't know whether to cry or scream, I just felt this feeling of having to make it back there to see her for the one last time. I had to phone my boss and tell her I would not be able to come to work tomorrow because my mother had passed away, she gave me her condolences and said take care while driving all that way. I packed my suit cases; I had to borrow the money to rent the car because I had used all my money to see her the day before, and now I had to go all the way back to my mom's funeral. It took me another five hours and I was going over the speed limit it was almost like I was going to miss her funeral. I had so many mixed emotions I could not explain how I was feeling, anger over my father, anger because my mom was gone, and Sadness. I wasn't going to go to the house my father was at I was going to go to a motel, but by the time I arrived it was visiting hours at the funeral home and I had to see my mom even though it had only been nine hours since I seen her, so I stopped at the 401 restaurant and change my clothes, I wore a gray dress with nylons, make up and earrings and jewelry, everything my father disapproved of. Again my father was a pillar of the community, so strong, yet grieving for this woman he said he loved. My father had no problems showing his emotional side, crying, shaking, and all the things he would never allow us to do or show. I can't believe this I said to myself, he does all these things behind closed doors and no one seems to care what happens to us kids, and he carries on as if nothing happened, and the woman he loved lays in front of him with tears in his eyes. Not even a day ago he tries to molest me and didn't even ask how she was when I seen her. The nurses said he hadn't been in to see her in a couple of days, and he had never allowed them to give her any pain medication. Doesn't that tell ya that he really loved her? After the funeral I went home. I was glad that I was gone from there and my mom was no longer in pain and suffering that he had put her through for so many years. Everything kept coming back to what my father had done before, and what he had tried to do the day my mom died. It won't get out of my head I don't want to live. Why, did this have to happen to me? There really is something wrong with me, I know there is, I can't put my finger on it but there's something wrong. My mother died of cancer, three different types, and the bastard had to live through three or four heart attacks, one that made a hole in his heart and he still didn't die before my mom, which I thought should have happened. I blame god, everyone and the world. My life was over. Life wasn't worth much at all, my mom, my friend, she is gone and I can't call her any more, so what have I got left to live for? My birth family, I can't find. The family I was adopted into never recognizes me and now my mother has passed away. My brother in my adoptive family never speaks to me and never recognizes me as his sister or even related to him. My so called father, all he wants is my body; he doesn't want to recognize me as his daughter or adoptive daughter and he can't seem to stop telling everyone what a bad person I am. So what do I have left? Several doctors have also said I would never live past 40 because of so many things that are wrong with me medically. At this point I had decided I might as well just live it out, because I would never live past 40 and that wasn't too far off.

I had my three days off of work and now it's time to go back. When I got back to work they had bought me flowers and a card with their condolences from all my colleagues and staff. It wasn't long after my mother's funeral I quit my job, it wasn't worth the frustration to me anymore, there was nothing left for me anyway.

After I left that job I became what they called a car jockey, transporting new and used cars from all over Ontario. I did this for a couple months, and one day I started having problems, my hair was falling out and not being able to staying awake, my friend from across the road came over after phoning several times with no success of keeping me awake. She took me to the hospital and they kept me there and found out that my Thyroid wasn't working right and called in a specialist from London Ontario. It took them six months to finally get the medication right in order for me to stay awake. After all this I became a taxicab driver that seemed a little better I could talk to people and listen to their problems and that made my problem seem a lot smaller and less important. I worked twelve hour shifts six or seven days a week it depended upon how many drivers they needed that day. It was my day off and I decided to go down to the mall and see if any of my friends were there. This one girl she came up to me, sat down and started talking to me, I didn't know her at all, never seen her before. As we talked I began to really like her, she was a nice girl. The way she had talked I knew she had been through some similar things as me but I did not tell her this, we seem to have hit it off, we began laughing over different things we were saying. Then I ask her, if she would like to come home with me and have dinner, she was a very hyper, girl she jumped up and down and said yes. We went back to my house and I made us some supper that is when she decided to tell me she was a runaway. My mouth dropped to the floor, I said; where did you run from, she said from child services they have me in a detention center that I feel I don't belong in, so I ran away, I told her I could get in trouble with having her here, I could even go to jail. She replied; call my caseworker she's really nice, she understands me. I said OK here's the phone, you dial the number and talk to her, then give me the phone for me to talk to your caseworker. She dialed the number and got a hold of her caseworker, immediately asked the caseworker if I could be her Foster parent, without asking me first. The caseworker asked me if I could or would go through the procedures to become the Foster parent for this girl, I replied I could, but I won't be accepted, I'm not a stable enough person to look after a girl in need like she was. I have never been stable enough even to have my own children, life sucks and I really don't want to live but I'm not going to be stupid and do something crazy. The caseworker said I will be over tomorrow we can sit down, talk about it and maybe fill out the papers, I agreed and asked if the girl could stay overnight with me, the caseworker replied you know you could be charged with harboring a runaway, but I will not charge you and yes we will leave her there for the night. We sat up half the night talking about her past and how she wanted her future to go. Man, did she ever sound like me and what I had gone through, but I never told her everything about me. I don't want everyone to know me, it frightens me.

The next day the caseworker came over and we sat at the kitchen table talking. I did not like caseworkers and I let her know that right off the bat. My anger came up real quick as she was explaining that I could be charged, I told her I'd rather kill her then talked to her, that's how bad I disliked children's services and anyone to do with the agency. After a while of talking she said you would be very good as a Foster parent for this girl and I'm almost positive you will be accepted as a provisional Foster parent. I replied if you really want to go through with this, I will as well. I'm willing enough to give it a try if she's willing to do her part as well. This is all new to me but I'm willing to help her and we seem to get along just great. The first month I received a check and I took it back to the agency and said I don't want this, if I'm volunteering to look after this child I should have money of my own to provide for her. They said, no we have to give you the money for supporting her, I said it's more than what I make at my job and it's definitely more than I pay for rent, well I will put it in a bank account for her they replied; know you can't do that, that is for you, groceries, toiletries, etc. rent all the things you need to pay for her. I reluctantly accepted because I had no choice.

My new Foster daughter and I got along well for a couple of months. Until she tested the rules then she got into a little bit of trouble again and had to go back to the detention center during the week, then she started to run away from there I would get a call at my work saying your daughter want you to pick her up, I knew there was something wrong then, because it was a Tuesday or Wednesday and she wasn't allowed out on most days. I would go, book off work and pick her up. I ask her what the problem was if she would only listen it wouldn't be so hard on her, she would start to cry and say I don't belong there. If you would only listen and do the right things you wouldn't end up in there, you would be staying here with me, I ask her what makes you do the things you do, her reply; I don't know that's just the way I am, I said to her that's not the way you are that's the way you chose to be and she said I guess you're right. Everyone has a path to lead in life and that path comes to a decision to go left or right meaning the right road or rough road and that rough road can get you in a lot of trouble, the right road isn't easy but you're not in trouble. That night after I finished talking with her and we went to bed, I started thinking what I had said to her, I just answered my own questions and knew from then on I would need to listen to my heart but that wasn't easy. Life throws a bunch of crap at you and I knew it was happening to her. She got up in the morning came over and gave me a big hug and said I love you, you are my mom. My reply was I'm your Foster mom I can not take away your real mom or replace her, I cannot do that. She said as far as I'm concerned you are my mom, Foster mom or not you have taught me a lot. I said all I'm doing is what I think is best. I don't know if I'm right or wrong, but I'm glad it is working for you. It wasn't too long after another caseworker came over and asked if I could take another Foster girl. I said sure if I can help, why not. Another child came along, the same age as the first and same name as the first. Now isn't that confusing? The two girls got along well, they had their little arguments between one another just like anyone else, and as far as I'm concerned they were normal children. The children were not as bad as I was told; at least I didn't think so. My second foster child was in trouble at school and thought that I was going to sit home babysitting, well that didn't happen. I marched her back to school and to the principal's office and ask why are you sending this child home, the incident happened at school and should be dealt with at the school, I need to work in order to support my family, I cannot be sitting at home doing your work. I feel she should be punished here, by sitting in your office until this is resolved. The principle agreed with me and she sat in the office until it was resolved. It didn't take long for her (the second Foster child) not to do what was causing the problem because she did not like sitting in the office, she preferred to sit at home which was not going to happen. She got angry with me about it and we sat down and talked. When I explained the whole thing to her she understood and it was fine from then on, there was no principal's office and no detentions for the rest of the time she lived with me. I guess I am not as bad as I thought I was, it boosted my morale and my confidence, and also taught me a lot of things, one social workers are not all that bad.

One day my fears came true, the girls were old enough to go out on their own, I hated the idea of them leaving, because I came to love the girls as if they were my own. I didn't go back into Foster parenting after that. I could not handle not seeing the children again, they have their lives to carry on and their families, and I have to carry on with my life as if nothing ever happened. This was a piece of my life that still haunts me, not knowing what has happened to the girls, how are they, are they doing well. I hear things here and there, from different people that have seen them, and it makes me wonder if I did any good or not, I do not know, I never hear from them or see them after the first couple years of them being gone. They live on their own with their friends.

Trying To Recognize What The Problem Is

I am on my own again no boyfriend, children, and no boarders. I am trying to sort out what is going on in my life. There is something wrong and I can't figure out what it is I don't want to live and the feeling is getting stronger, if I'm not working 24 hours seven days a week, my brain starts thinking of different ways to end my life. I know this is not healthy, but my brain just won't stop, that is why I'd ask psychiatrists in the past to give me shock treatments to fry my brain so I did not have to think again of my past. Of course they have refused, saying it would only black out my short memory not my long term memory and then eventually it would come back anyways. I also know that there would be many people that miss me if I should die, but in my head at this time there is nobody to help me or be my friend, even my true friends in my head were against me. Doctors, lawyers, and teachers they were all there, but to me they were only doing a job for the money not to help the person out. So I have to figure out how I'm going to live the rest of my life, this isn't going to be easy. I went to another social worker and she didn't seem to know how to help me. So I went to yet another she also said there's nothing that she could do for me because I know the answers, I wouldn't be coming to you if I knew the answers I told her. And then one day a friend of mine came by, that was having basically the same problem with depression and not wanting to live, and said there's a program in Tucson Arizona and another one in San Antonio Texas that deals with codependence. Well this was surprising maybe this is what is wrong with me. I ask all sorts of questions, phone numbers, how long the program was, who pays, and what it consisted of, and of course how do you get there. She said; it is minimum 30 days, you have to fly from Detroit, and the Canadian government pays for it. What! The Canadian government pays for this! You mean I can get some help. She replied; yes, she also wanted to know if I would schedule the same time as her, I said no, I want to go, but not when she was going. If I am going to tell anybody part of my life, I'm certainly not going to tell someone I know, may use it against me, and she is the type of person that would.

There were a lot of things going on right at that time. I had a search going on to find part of my birth family and they had wrote back to me and said they had found my baby brother. I was excited, scared, and a mixture of feelings I had never felt before. I didn't know how to accept this, I didn't want to cry because you know what happens to people that cry, they fall apart and lose all sense of reality and may not come back also it was never an option when I was little, crying was forbidden. So crying isn't going to be on the top the list for me, I'm not going to lose it, I have come close but had the ability to stop. I put off going to San Antonio because I wanted to meet my baby brother. I talked with a friend of mine Hazel and she said we can make it a weekend trip with the whole family and that way I can be there to support you. Hazel is my friend, she has always been there for me and now she is willing to take her family all the way down to Toronto for all of us to meet my birth brother. She talked with me and explained to me why I felt the mixed feelings, which helped me a lot and helped me understand. The day finally came when we all jumped into the van and went off to meet my brother. He had sent a photo so we would know what he looked like, but that didn't help much because the picture had been an older one of years before and he did not look the same. I'm anxiously waiting in the motel coffee shop and I see this very tall young man, saying that might be him. Hazel and the children said; no they didn't think so. The children went up to the room just to see if he went to my room and knocked on the door, but it wasn't him. The kids came running down and said we seen your brother, really! He is here? They said yes, and then pointed at this very large bearded man, I started to laugh, and that cannot be my brother. He is too tall, he is three times the size I am, and it can't be him, it must be a mistake. I started to laugh when this big man walked up to me and said you must be my sister. We sat and talked for a long time but he never told me that he was just out of jail. And I won't get into all this discussion of my birth brother, because that is another story all on its own. After visiting him for a while and exchanging different things that have happened in our lives, we parted and said goodbye. We saw each other off and on after that.

After we got home Hazel suggested how she could help me out, she went out and bought several books, videos, and things pertaining to children. We sat down and went through many of them, to teach me how children were supposed to be and how they react and the fun that children are supposed to have not the destruction I had. There was an awful lot of things in my life I didn't know, mostly how children have fun.

Approximately a year after I had met my birth brother a doctor had scheduled me for surgery on my left jaw, it needed to be repaired. My TMJ joint needed to have a piece put in, to stop it from clicking and hurting. The surgeon wanted to do the other side at a later date. I have not yet had that done. That had to be a funny experience even though there was pain, because I came out of the surgery and my friend hazel and her family were there. The hospital cafeteria brought my supper in and we all started to laugh, they had given me pork chops to eat, I couldn't even open my mouth far enough to put a straw in for a drink let alone eating pork chops. I finally got that surgery over and started feeling better, they never gave me any physiotherapy to make my jaw work better, so I had to learn all on my own.

I was looking for a new job, the one I was doing involved driving a kind of truck full of the town's gazette newspaper and fliers, and I was working day and night with a couple hours off in between deliveries. I finally found one for a pet store driving their truck and stocking the shelves in her two stores. The owner asked me to come in for an interview, well it happened to be when I just got off work from the newspaper, so I was all dirty and covered with printing ink, but that didn't matter. I thought that I might as well go in even though I was dirty because the job I was applying for was in a warehouse. After about fifteen minutes of the interview she hired me, and asked me if I could start the next day. I told her I had to give my previous job two weeks notice, but I would work at both jobs for that two weeks, if she agreed. She agreed and set a schedule for me. I worked there for approximately four months. I worked in a warehouse filled with cans and bags of cat and dog food. She would always order the skids to be 6 ft. high. I told her that I would not be able to reach the top because I was only four foot eleven in height. I went to work this one day and decided OK I will climb up on the 6 ft. skid, what a mistake. I fell off headfirst to the cement floor below, no one else worked there so I was by myself. I must've been unconscious for a while, when I come too I could not walk, the pain in my back was so bad. I crawled over to the van and managed to lock the doors in the warehouse by holding on and pulling myself up. I drove very slowly over to the store where my boss was and ask her to drive me to the hospital. She said yes what happened and I told her, as we were going up to the hospital she said "I have to go to the states to pick up a puppy, so I will let you out here " I said OK. I went into the hospital and the doctors ask is this compensation or did you fall on your own. I replied it happened at work. They filled out some papers and sent that off to the workmen's compensation board and ask where my boss was that she had papers that she needed to be filled out as well, I told them where she was. When I went back to work the next day I told her the doctor said it had to be light duty but I would not be back to work I'm going to quit, but I did not want to leave her stuck and agreed to stay working until she found someone. The compensation board got a hold of her and she lied to them, she told them she knew nothing of the accident and that she dropped me off at the hospital to visit a friend when that wasn't the case. She told me she was not going to pay to a large sum to compensation just because someone gets hurt. The compensation board turned around and charged her with not having proper coverage for her employees and a fine. It must have been high, because she sold the store. I never received anything for the accident, because they said there was no witness, but they believed in me, I had severely injured my back, and from the papers my doctor sent in to the compensation. The report said I had four disks in my back that were injured, three bulging, and one with a tear in it. So this job didn't last long, the shortest job I think I ever had. It's bad to think that your boss would lie about an injured employee, but I guess it happens. The doctors told me, it more than likely would heal on its own but it would take time, it hasn't yet. The doctor said I could not sit for any more than twenty minutes or stand for any more than twenty minutes.

Hazel and her husband decided they would hire me to do some lawn maintenance for the company. I enjoyed doing that, and it was outside work. I had worked for another landscaping company before and knew what I had to do. Hazel and I became very good friends and still are to this day. I would be able to call her up anytime and talk, she helped me through so many times of stress and uncertainty and sometimes when I didn't want to live any longer but I never told her. She has stood by me for a long time. Hazel did a lot of counseling with me, even though she was a friend. She made me understand several things in my life that were not right and helped me to help myself. She was my angel, and didn't even know it.

I met this guy when I was a provisional Foster parent; he was a volunteer driver for child services. He was a very nice man his name was George, and every time I seen him at the coffee shop, or he seen me we would stop in and have a coffee, not thinking of anything else, other than being friends. I made sure that he was not married, because I was not going to split up a family. He told me he was still married, but they had separated with no intentions of getting back together. I don't mind being friends with people, but I don't want their wives to think that I'm going out with their husband, when the relationship is just friendship. I wanted to make sure he was telling me the truth, I will have my daughter come in to meet you, I said that would be great, I would love to meet her. This way it gave me a chance to find out if the truth was being told. My last relationship neglected to tell me he was married to two other women. We continued stopping in for coffee with each other, this went on for several months. We didn't ask where each other lives and we never went to each other houses it's just a coffee shop friendship. Then one day I asked George if he would like to go out for supper, he agreed I gave him my address. The day came for us to go out to supper, but I was gone.

The Day I Had Been Praying For All My Life Had Finally Come

January 1991 a phone call came, saying my father had died. He had taken a massive heart attack beside his car. At first they thought he had been murdered, and I felt fear in my heart and body, that they may come after me, thinking I might have murdered him, but I knew deep down inside they could not do that because I was six hours away when he died, but the fear was still there, and that maybe somehow he would have made it look like it was me. I didn't have a long to make it down there for the funeral; it was within the day or two of his death. I had to go, I had to see and make sure he was dead. I couldn't believe this man had died, I thought it was a hoax and when I did get there, my mind didn't want to believe, and it was like a dream. I started to laugh hysterically, then said to myself it looks good on you, you bastard, why couldn't you have died sooner, before mom. I was angry I didn't have the guts to tell him off before he died, I needed to do that, but I couldn't. I couldn't bring myself to telling him how

I really felt, my mind and body wouldn't do it, because I knew if I was in the same room as him, he would try having sex with me all over again, the same as he did when my mother died. After the funeral I came back home and went to Hazel's house, where we stood out in the driveway talking about how angry I was about not telling him off. Now that he is gone maybe I can get on with my life. I was not in the will, so I wasn't expecting very much at all, when my brother called and asked me if I would like our father's car. I very much would like that car, I said that you know dad he didn't want me to have anything, he replied I know he didn't, but I can get you the car if you want it, or need it. Yes I do need I said, I have a truck that needs to be replaced. Within a couple of months I got the car and I finally got my mom's sewing machine that meant so much to me. I'm finally free of the men that destroyed my life.

George and I had not seen each other since dad had died. So I thought maybe it was over, our friendship that is, but it wasn't

He just didn't know when I would be home to get a hold of me. Then I left for Texas to co-dependency course, I didn't explain to George what the co-dependency course was or why I was going, for the first time in my life I thought I could make my own decisions and not have to worry about backlash of some kind. I didn't know George that well at the time, so I was not going to tell him anything, until I learned what he was like. I was there for a whole month. I learned a lot, even things that I didn't want to know came out. I learned how to control my anger, and to stop from exploding at the least little thing. It wasn't easy for me to be in a group setting, I didn't get along well with groups. My thoughts were people don't need to know who I am or what has happened to me in my past, because they would think that if me and likely think I am lying. I didn't have a lot of time to think because it was from early in the morning till late at night. If we were good that week, meaning we didn't explode or go off the wall, we would have a surprise at the end of the week and go to the boardwalk or to the Mexican market, were they sold items for less than half of what you would pay here. I ended up only going on one excursion over the course of the month, because I could not handle the group setting and left and went to my room. I met a girl there she was one of the nurses, we would go for walks and talk for hours, we became friends and stayed friends even after I came home to Canada. She came to visit a couple of times and that was nice, but I haven't seen her for a long time, she was to be married and I have not heard from her since. When I came home from the course, I tried to stay with the weekly meetings but they soon disappeared no one was going. I can say it did help me with some of life's problem. I know, it didn't help me out with the problems I was having about my past, I don't know what to call the feelings. It's really hard to explain how a person feels when their past has been as brutal as mine, one minute you're fine, life seems very good, you're happy, sun shining, and then the thunder will roll, in a split second everything would change to, angry, wanting to die, wishing I wasn't born. What I did learn is people have a co-dependency to each other whether it is for good or bad. Needing to be acknowledged seems to be a priority in most cases, whether it is good or bad. I believe I came out of this with my eyes open and not shut, like a lot of other times that I had been in counseling, believing it could work for me if I'd tried. It has worked for me in a lot of ways. I don't know whether it's because my father is deceased now and I can get on with my life or the counseling I have received over the years is finally working.

George and I are getting closer together every day. We go out for dinner and go on trips, and we don't argue, we discuss things, with no yelling, screaming, hitting. It is so nice not to be afraid. He treats me like a person and he is always stood beside me through everything, not once has he asked or questioned what has happened in my past and most of all he believes me. George came to me one day and asked me if I was going to go out with him, or not, he thought I was giving him mixed messages, he was not sure what I meant. I was shocked when he asked me, because I thought we would just be friends, and I didn't think I was his type to get into a long lasting relationship. I was excited but also afraid, because my ex husband was still around and I began to fear that he would cause problems, I explained everything to George, what he had done in the past and why I was a little leery of going out with someone else, but George made me feel safe and assured me nothing would happen. My ex husband would not hurt me anymore, he said; not as long as I'm around. That made me feel safe with George and he did treat me wonderfully. He didn't try to shower me with gifts, and flowers like a lot of men do. He just told it as it was, straight to the point. I came up with this idea of going Toronto for the weekend, not thinking that we would be in the same motel room. When we got to Toronto we went in to the motel and the desk clerk asked me, will that be a queen size bed or two double beds, I turned red George started laughing and said whatever you want, it is your decision. I didn't know what to do. I started thinking; well he's likely got his pajamas, just like me. I decided that the same room would be OK, but different beds I think I could handle this, so I told the clerk two double beds.

When we got to the room I sat down on one of the beds and George sat on the other and we discussed this is just for a vacation and don't try anything funny. We both understood each other and we went out on the town. That night we both got ready for bed and went to bed with no problem, but when I woke up in the morning George was sitting by the bed looking at me. He said I hope you don't mind I was just watching you sleep, I didn't feel scared or upset I knew this man was for me. He asked me, can I kiss you, my reply; yes you may. I've heard from several people that if it's true love, on the first kiss firecrackers go off, you see stars and you just know it's the right one. He has the softest, velvety lips I have ever kissed. I knew with that kiss, that very first kiss he was the man of my dreams, and we were going to live the rest of our lives together. November fifteenth 1991 his daughter and him moved in. he has never raised his hand to me not like almost every man I ever met. He talks with me, he doesn't talk down to me, and he does not tell me what to do. I don't tell him what to do or nag at him every five seconds over stupid little things. We get along just like friends that's because we are friends. In July fifth, 1996 we decided to get married, we didn't have a big wedding we just had some family; on my side it was just some friends, I had no family other than my friends. I can't believe that finally I can be happy. I have told George a lot of things that's happened in my past but I haven't told all yet, maybe someday I will be able to tell him.

I started to look for my biological family again, but was hesitant because of my younger brother I have already met. George said to me that not all people are alike, and not to think my other siblings would be the same. I began searching and searching finally I got an answer. The call came in saying they had found my father but he was deceased. And then a couple days later another call came in saying they found my oldest brother but he was also deceased, I felt heavy, was overset with feelings and that's when I knew I had other feelings that I had never experienced. The feelings I had were of sadness, and those feelings I was never allowed to have, I always held them back, stuffed them away so I did not have to feel, I was safer that way. I received another phone call, saying your brother is not deceased after all, we made a mistake. I hung up the phone and ran out to the garage where George was, jumping up and down and howling, he was laughing so hard and saying, calm down! I can't understand what you're saying. I finally got calmed down and told him they had found my brother that he wasn't dead. George said well that is really good, so when do you get to talk to him, I said I don't know they gave him my phone number for him to call me when he is ready. Then I began to have another feeling, the feeling of being afraid of someone I didn't know, even though it was my brother the fear was there and I didn't know how to handle it. Children's services said that they would set up meetings between siblings so you would get to know them, before you would have to be on your own, but that didn't happen. There were no meetings, you just dealt with it. The next day the phone call came in it was my brother I didn't know what to say, he was talking so fast I didn't hear what he said he was also excited. He asked me where I was living and if he could come see me, of course I'm going to tell him, he's my brother. I gave him the address and said goodbye see you tomorrow. He and his wife had to drive six hours or seven hours to come to where I live because they live so far away. It was raining that day when they pulled in the driveway and I opened the door and just stood there staring at him. It was like looking in a mirror, the only thing different he was a man and I'm a woman. The rain was coming down very hard and we're still standing there, I hollered come on in get out of the rain, and they came in. I didn't know what type of feelings I could call it, because

I never had these feelings before, maybe a fear, happiness, excitement, or everything all lumped together, and I don't know. We sat down at the table He had brought pictures of when I was smaller, before I was adopted. There were a lot of feelings going on inside of me that I didn't know how to respond to. Then he and his wife told me of my two other brothers, they know where they were, and gave me their phone numbers. Then I told them I knew our youngest brother and I know where he was, but he didn't have a phone number. There is only two left that I had to find, one more brother and my one and only sister. My brother wanted me to come back home with him and his wife, and that he would drive his vehicle, a feeling came over me that I could not explain to him, I had to tell him, no! I would not have an escape route in place, if anything went wrong. If I come I will come in my vehicle with my husband. All I could think of is, you don't know this man, you cannot go with him, and he could hurt you. I didn't want anyone to know that I was afraid; I was not going to ever be stuck without a way out. I started thinking, why would you think your brother would hurt you, what is wrong with you to think that way, I didn't know what to think I didn't know what to say. I phoned my friend Hazel and told her, we went out for coffee and she explained things to me, that made me feel a lot better, but the feelings were still there. I didn't trust my own feelings, so how could I trust this man that is supposed to be my brother; he is a stranger to me. I didn't know how to get rid of these feelings; I guess I just have to live with it like I did when I was younger.

They had left and went back to their home, and I had to call my other brothers, but I was afraid, afraid of what they might think of me, because I believed in hiding all emotions, and myself if I could, if I could be invisible it would have made everything better but that is not realistic. Now there are more people that are going to know me, I cannot have others knowing me, I worried every day that people would find out about my past, it is a secret I have kept all my life and now that I am older, I don't want people to know. I don't have the strength to deal with more feelings for brothers and sisters, I only have enough strength for my husband and friends, most people that already know me, know I'm not a bad person, and at least I think they do. How am I going to deal with this? After my father had died I thought I would be feeling like a normal person, but what does a normal person feel like, you would think at my age I would know, but I don't know. My search for normalcy was just beginning, even though I went to different counselors, psychiatrists, psychologists and doctors, which none could help me in my quest. In all the years of being clear of the turmoil, sexual and physical abuse, I still couldn't find a reason to live. I had made up my mind that I would not commit suicide, but deep down inside I couldn't understand why I would want to live in this world there was no reason for my being here, I was still a nothing, the white people didn't want me, the native people didn't want me, I am not white, I am not native, so they call that Métis and even them I didn't fit with. My biological brother's all told me; our mother is native and our grandfather is full native. On my oldest brother's birth certificate it said native, I seen it with my own eyes. Native of affairs tried to help in the search but came up with too many names the same, what we had to do is find the band number and his middle name. I still have to find my sister and my other brother. Finally I received another phone call from children's services, we found your brother and they said they gave him my number, so he would call when he felt comfortable enough to call. I went through the same thing as I did with my first call, all excited and scared. Now there is just one more to find and that is my sister. I wonder if I'm going to find her, girls you know change their name after marriage. It took only a week later from finding my brother, I received another call saying they found my sister. Well that didn't take long. But I'm more excited to talk to my sister than all the rest, questions are racing through my head, does she look like me, is she taller than me, does she think the same way as I do, and will she like me or will she turn me away. These are all the things I have to deal with. I'm not sure I can do it, but I have to. Something inside of me is driving me to find them, I don't know why, maybe because they are my biological family, even though I was raised in another family. Maybe I think it's going to be different and it's going to make me have a reason to live, because right now I have none. My sister finally phoned me, I was excited she didn't sound the same as I had expected. I have a deep voice and she had this high pitched feminine voice, but I felt almost attached to her as we talked on the phone. It wasn't like when I talk to the boys, it is different, and I could feel the connection between the two of us. I ask her if I can come and see her and she replied; yes we made the appointment and I went to meet her. She is a wonderful person and I think the world of her, I don't ever want her to go out of my life. I don't want the boys to go out of my life either, but the feeling toward my sister is different from the feeling toward my brothers. I don't believe there is a connection between me and my brothers like there is with my sister, there was with the boys in the beginning but not now. Don't get me wrong my brothers are wonderful people too and I think the world of them, but it's different for women.

The Last Chapter In This Book Of My Life And How I Learned To Be Normal

George and I love each other very much, we have no arguments, but we do have our discussions. We used to go out into the garage and stay there in to wee hours of the morning making all sorts of wood products to sell and give away as presents. We get along very well; we do everything together as friends, and a team. I have not told him everything about my past, but I will here shortly, because things are starting to spin out of control again, and he deserves to know. I'm a little afraid of telling him just in case it will scare him away, but I have to take my chances and tell him.

George was offered a buyout from where he worked, he decided he had enough of that work and accepted the package. We went out and bought a truck and started traveling across Ontario. We traveled for a month all over. It was wonderful, exciting and something I had not done before. We started a business together doing commercial cleaning. I was on the disability at the time. I turned in everything that disability ask for, so they couldn't say that I was committing fraud, there was more paperwork for the disability then there was work in the company. I got so discouraged they wanted me to tell them when I needed to buy a vacuum and then they had to approve it. It didn't seem like it was my own company, it seemed like the government had even taken that over, so where is my freedom, I guess I don't have any, I never did, but I will someday I hope. I still had that little glimmer of hope, that someday I will be my own person, and not be a puppet for everyone else. Things seem to be getting harder to live again. I kept telling my friends when they asked, are you going to be all right? I promised them, I would not commit suicide or do anything stupid, so that tied my hands so I couldn't commit suicide even if I wanted, because I made a promise and I could not break it, but that didn't stop me from not wanting to live. I still had no reason to live, even though I had God, George and Hazel in my life to help make my life happier, it didn't stop the feelings I felt. We decided that we were going to move to some place we both wanted to be and enjoyed, because we did not like it where we were. I didn't like it because I could never get a fulltime job, I always worked three or four jobs at one time just to make ends meet, and I was tired of it. So we moved from south western Ontario to south eastern Ontario on January sixth 2000 we left at 6:00 at night with a full truck and headed out leaving everything behind, family and friends to start anew. We didn't know exactly where we would be living, just that we wanted to be in a happy place. We found a little town the next day that we wanted to stay at and started looking around for an apartment that we could call our temporary home, until we could buy our own house. We found our apartment and moved in on the tenth of January 2000. It didn't take too long for me to get a job, and George also found a part time job that he liked. Within a week I was working fulltime, boy did that ever feel good. To have a fulltime job was like having Christmas to me. We were tired from the move, and then going back into work after being off for so long.

I went to a temporary agency and they had me working fulltime even though it was classified as a part time job. It was more than fulltime really because they would call me in a couple hours after I had gone home from one location and sent me to another. We were literally starting new.

The temporary agency placed me in a fantastic job I loved it, it was called the continental shift. They told me that this would never turn into a fulltime job because there was a freeze on hiring at that plant, but I still brought home a nice paycheck. Then I started to learn the temporary agency was charging more than what I was bringing home, I did not know this when I started. I was disappointed in the news, but had decided that this would do for now until I could find a fulltime permanent job I knew I could do it, I just needed time. The day came when they made a mistake and asked me if I would go to work at this other plant that it could possibly turn into a fulltime permanent position, and I answer yes. This is what I wanted; the time had come for me to have a fulltime job permanent. I started working there on the Monday morning and fell right in love with it. Part of the plant was union and the other half was nonunion. I was still classified as a temporary worker until I worked their sixteen weeks, it didn't take long for the sixteen weeks to go by. They hired me after my sixteen weeks was up, they liked my work. They said I had good work ethics, which made me very proud.

I can't believe what I've went through and finally I feel the world has made me happy for once in my life. The happiness started to slide as the days went by, people started to trigger feelings from my past. I started not being able to sleep properly, not wanting to go into work because of another person that work there. Now my world is starting to fall apart again, what is wrong with me, I have not asked for any help here, because I thought I could get away with doing it on my own, and with the help of my husband, but it didn't work. I finally had to sit down and tell my husband what had happened so many years ago, and what I was feeling like, I didn't want to live again. I made a decision that I would go to a counselor and if that didn't work I would be gone. Not gone from the job of gone from this earth. Life had dealt me a hand that I had to work at, but how long do I have to work at this. No one should have to work all their life for nothing, that's how I felt. My world was falling down and there was nothing I could do to stop it. I went to the nurse at the plant and talk to her; she referred me to a counselor and gave me some time off. If I didn't get this resolved, I would lose my job, I have not lost a job in my life that I didn't want leave. I went to the counselor and she asked me what I was feeling. I couldn't tell her how I was feeling other than I really didn't want to live. I told her about the girl at work that reminded me of the man that raped me when I was younger, on several occasions. She had me signing some papers and asked me if I would like a cup of tea with her I said no thank you, as she was making herself a tea she said; were you sexually molested when you were a child. I was stunned that she would ask me such a question. I said, yes and responded why would you ask a person that? Then I started to feel frightened that someone else knew. This was strange to me. This woman really knows what she's doing. Maybe there is some help here, she could see it in my responses, and none of the others had seen it, but she does. Now maybe I can get some help, and maybe learn to be normal. She said to me, I really don't deal with this type of problem. Would you consider going to the sexual assault center? I said, I've never been sexually assaulted, that wouldn't have anything to do with me. She kinda chuckled yes it does she replied. If you were molested you were sexually assaulted. I was stunned I didn't connect the two. She said that she would get a hold of them, but I would have to go in on my own, she said that's how it works, the client has to make the first call to show they are interested in the help. I said I could do that, I think. After having the conversation with her I felt more confused that molest as a child and sexual assault meant the same thing. I felt angry. I was always angry when I heard that someone was sexually assaulted, I knew what that meant, but being molested that was a different story. She said to me on my next visit that she would not leave me in the condition I was in until I got help, this was also different. She showed concern and compassion, I never seen this from a counselor before, other than the one that helped me with my alcohol and drug problem. I went down to the center I was terrified when I was going through the doors because there were men out in front and I thought that they would know where I was going. My husband was with me at the time so that helped me as well, he never came in with me he stayed in the truck. When I went through the office door there was this lady sitting at a computer and talking on the phone, I said hi is this the sexual assault center? She replied yes may I help you? I said; I was told to come down here to get some information about sexual abuse and incest. This woman didn't even look at me funny, like I wasn't strange for asking, now that is strange I was totally confused and not understanding what was happening. What does this mean? It must be the right thing to do, because things are so different, people are being nice to me that is not normal. I've always been afraid of people. The lady had told me that I would have to phone to make an appointment for counseling, if that's what I wanted to do. So I took the package home and read all the information in it and made my decision that I would try these people out. I spoke with my husband and told him everything and that was easy. He's had nothing but compassion, love and caring through this whole process, he has stood beside me all the way. That drew me closer to my husband.

I made the phone call and ask for an appointment, they told me they'd call me back with the time and date. It didn't take too long maybe a week or two. Then I got another phone call ask me if I would come in for an interview, when I got there, there were two ladies sitting in chairs the one was very quiet and the other was asking the questions. I was really suspicious of the first woman there she seldom looked at me and sat very quiet she might have asked me one question I can't remember now, the first thing that went through my head, she's a cop and if I say too much I will be in trouble or someone else would. The other lady she was very nice understanding, compassionate and asked; would I go into a group for counseling my reply is yes I will try it. I told her I had never been in group counseling and I didn't know how I would be. Then came the day when I went to group counseling, and the next day I went to one on one, counseling. I was very quiet in the group there was a lot of people there that I didn't know and was not sure of. Are these people going to judge me, or like me, ridicule what I have to say, these things were going on in my brain as I sat there listening to each one of them. Maybe these people think I'm crazy and maybe they think I think they're crazy but I don't. It took me about a month or maybe a little less to start talking to these people, now that I know they went through the same thing as I did and are trying to get to be normal just like me. They're not bad people they're very nice people and I am proud to be a part of their group. We became friends and that meant a lot to me and still does. I went through the phase one. Then I went through a phase two, that even taught me even more of why I was acting and feeling the way I was. Then I went through phase three the last phase, by this time I knew why I was feeling the way I had, and how to change, how to be normal and how to stop the bad feelings of not wanting to live and how to be grounded and not hold on to the previous lifestyle, and most of all the nightmares are gone. I still have to work on not being afraid of people, I'm not afraid of one person at a time; it's the group of people, even if I know them. It was the best thing that ever happened to me and the best counselors there ever was. If all counselors could be the same all the survivors would be able to heal properly. There are all different types of counselor you just have to go to the right ones. My one on one counselor that I had been seeing while going to groups as well, had an understanding and knew what I went through. She had compassion and understanding that I didn't understand at that point. She'd let me answer my own questions and believe me I had the right answers, but she knew how to steer it in the right direction and not let me ramble. We would walk around the block and I would talk about everything that happened in my past, there was no judgment toward me, I was just me. Even though I gave her an ultimatum that if I didn't get better within three months I was going to commit suicide, she had no judgment. She is a special counselor in my heart and always will be; she is fantastic with what she does and has a heart of gold. I would recommend her to everyone and also her colleagues, there all so wonderful they helped me. Now that I've gone through everything now I can go one with my life and that is how I decided to write this book to be published. I have written it many times before but not to be published. I wrote it out of anger, then I wrote out of the "poor me's" and then "the world owes me", now this one that is published for healing and it has worked for me.

Since 2000 I have become a person of my own being, and everything that has happened since that day we moved here, has been for the better. I don't think geographical moves are always the answer, but this one was a good one. Even though I am medically not sound, mentally I am. It's like going to a Mechanic for television repair you wouldn't do that, you would go for your car repair, and the television you would go to a television repairman/ repair woman, well go to the right counselor for the right thing and the healing will begin.

I would love to become a counselor to help all the survivors of child abuse and sexual abuse but I don't know if my medical condition would allow me.

So this is all the different things that have happened to me over the years and some people they call me a miracle and as far as I am concerned now, I am a miracle. I have a fractured skull that happened when I was a child, that never healed, a brain tumor, lymphoma stage four, both knees had surgery, both elbows had surgery, a broken nose from a man in a bar, my left jaw had surgery to put a piece in, off and on diabetic, I laugh at that one too, and now the latest thing a heart attack and three stents put in my heart.

Now this is the end of my book. I hope you enjoyed it. I enjoyed the healing that came from writing this. It wasn't the easiest thing in my life to do, going through counseling for so many years, and I still may have to go again, but I know now most of the ways to help myself.

Commentary

November 23, 2006.

TODAY: Deb is a vibrant, others' centered, compassionate, beautiful woman with many friends and an adoring family!

The path she walked to get here was so hard! As a very young child Deb was severely victimized. No part of her was sacrosanct. The dim lights of hope she received from her adopted mother, grandmother and others never gave her an escape. Her own initial efforts were laden with further tragedy and grief.

In 1987 I was a social worker and met Deb through work. Over time she, and now her husband George, have become dear friends of our whole family. Deb is respected by my husband as both a friend and a former employee. She was looked up to and now is towered over and adored by my children. In my heart she has become my little sister.

After some time of interacting with Deb I came to realize that: "This isn't just some 'tough broad' who'd just as soon beat me up or take a knife to me. This is a beautiful and vulnerable young woman who is trying to climb out of a dark hole so deep it's nigh unto impossible for any human!!"

And yet she was trying. Deb was someone who had stepped onto a platform that holds a weigh scale. On one side is a survivor. On the other side is an individual who is healed; heart, mind, body and soul. When I first met Deb the scale was tipped heavily on the survivor side. I've watched that weigh scale rock back and forth as Deb has come to know Jesus as her Lord and grown in His love. In stages, she has faced demon after demon from her past as her heart, mind and soul were able to bear it. The weigh scale is now so heavily tipped on the 'healed side' that Deb has begun to actively help others with their healing. Every time I think on it my heart shouts for joy!!

There is something very special about Deb. She is as grounded and real as she ever was. Inside she is still that tough, dangerous woman who had eyes that dared me to play a "fake" card so she could have an excuse to "beat the shit out of me". That woman learned that some people will dare to be genuine and vulnerable; that true friendship can last and be trusted through the good, the bad and the ugly. She learned that, in the midst of struggles, incredible times of joy can be made. Those joys are treasures, kept in a chest, to be pulled out and laughingly reviewed with friends as often as possible. That even when you think you've over come your past there may be more challenges ahead. But that's OK, because God has granted you a healed foundation, inner love and strength, and loving family and friends.

Above all Deb is someone to look up to. She is someone who emulates genuine character, tenacity, hope and joy. Good on ya Deb!!!

Hazel

www.ingramcontent.com/pod-product-compliance
Ingram Content Group UK Ltd.
Pitfield, Milton Keynes, MK11 3LW, UK
UKHW021053270726
13967UKWH00012B/640